AF454100

NAKANO TAKEKO

THE LAST OF THE SAMURAI

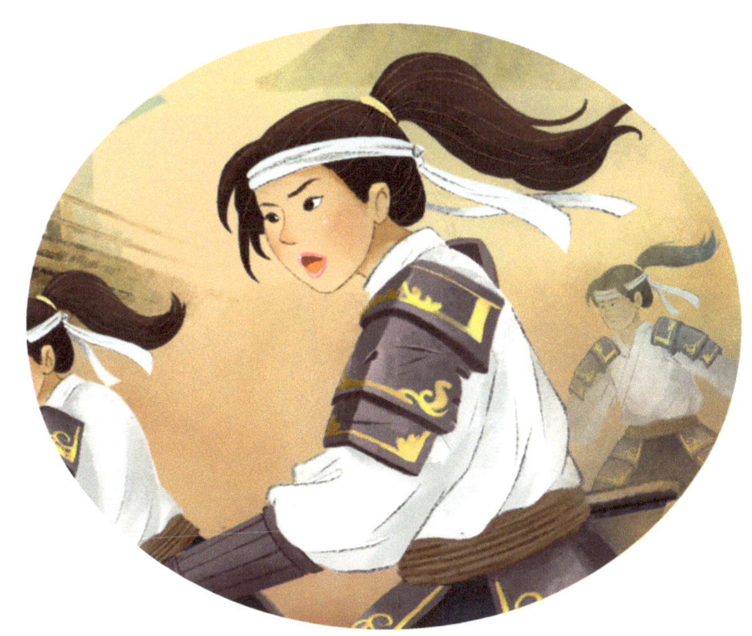

Written by
AIDA ZACIRAGIC

Illustrated by
HAO NGUYEN

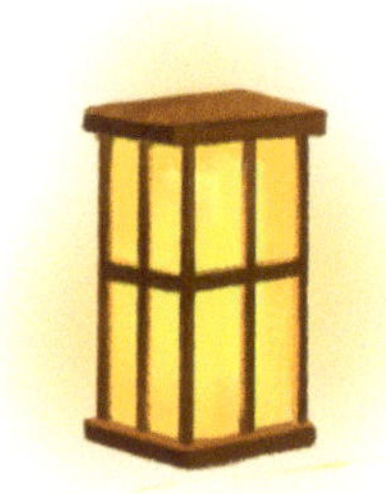

Title
Nakano Takeko - The Last of the Samurai

Written by
Aida Zaciragic

Illustrated by
Hao Nguyen

Names: Zaciragic, Aida, author.
Title: Nakano Takeko the last of samurai / Aida Zaciragic.
Description: Sweden: Aida Zaciragic, 2024. | Summary: A children's biography about one of the last samurai, Nakano Takeko.

Identifiers: ISBN: 978-91-531-2650-8 (hardcover) | 978-91-531-2646-1 (paperback) | 978-91-531-2648-5 (eBook)

Subjects: LCSH Takeko, Nakano--Juvenile literature. | Samurai--Juvenile literature. | Women heroes--Biography--Juvenile literature. | Military art and science--Japan--Juvenile literature. | Soldiers--Japan--Juvenile literature. | BISAC JUVENILE NONFICTION / Biography &; Autobiography / Historical | JUVENILE NONFICTION / Biography &; Autobiography / Women
Classification: LCC DS827.S3 .T35 Z33 2024 | DDC 952.02/092--dc23

"I WOULD NOT DARE TO
COUNT MYSELF AMONG THE
FAMOUS WARRIORS—EVEN
THOUGH I SHARE THE SAME
BRAVE HEART."

NAKANO TAKEKO

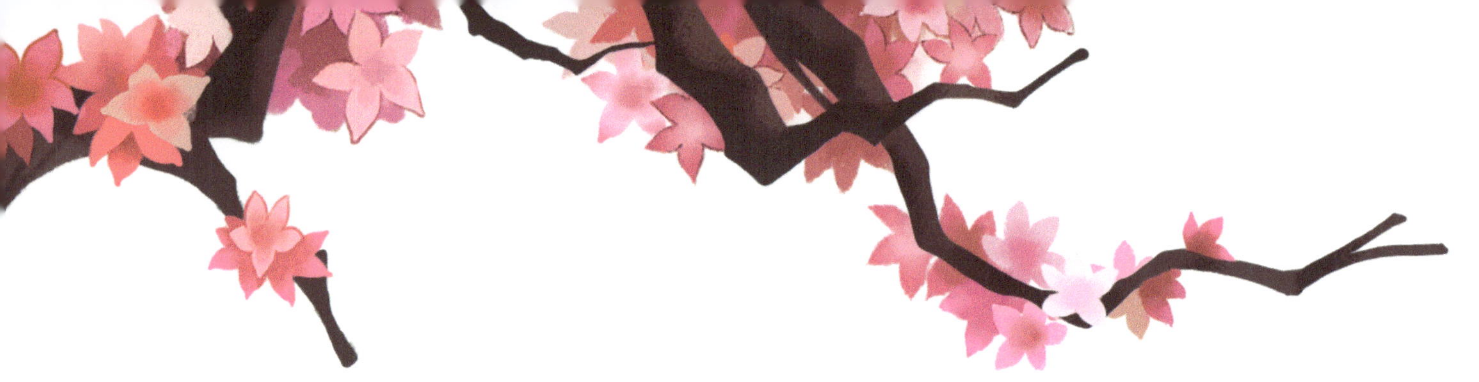

The girl who would later become one of the **BRAVEST WOMEN** in the world was born into a samurai family in Edo.

She grew up with her mom, dad, younger sister Yuko, and little brother Toyonori.

Takeko's family belonged to the Aizu clan, which was loyal to the Shogun.

Since she grew up in a samurai family, Takeko was surrounded by the bravest samurai of that time.

From an early age, she knew she would become a samurai one day.

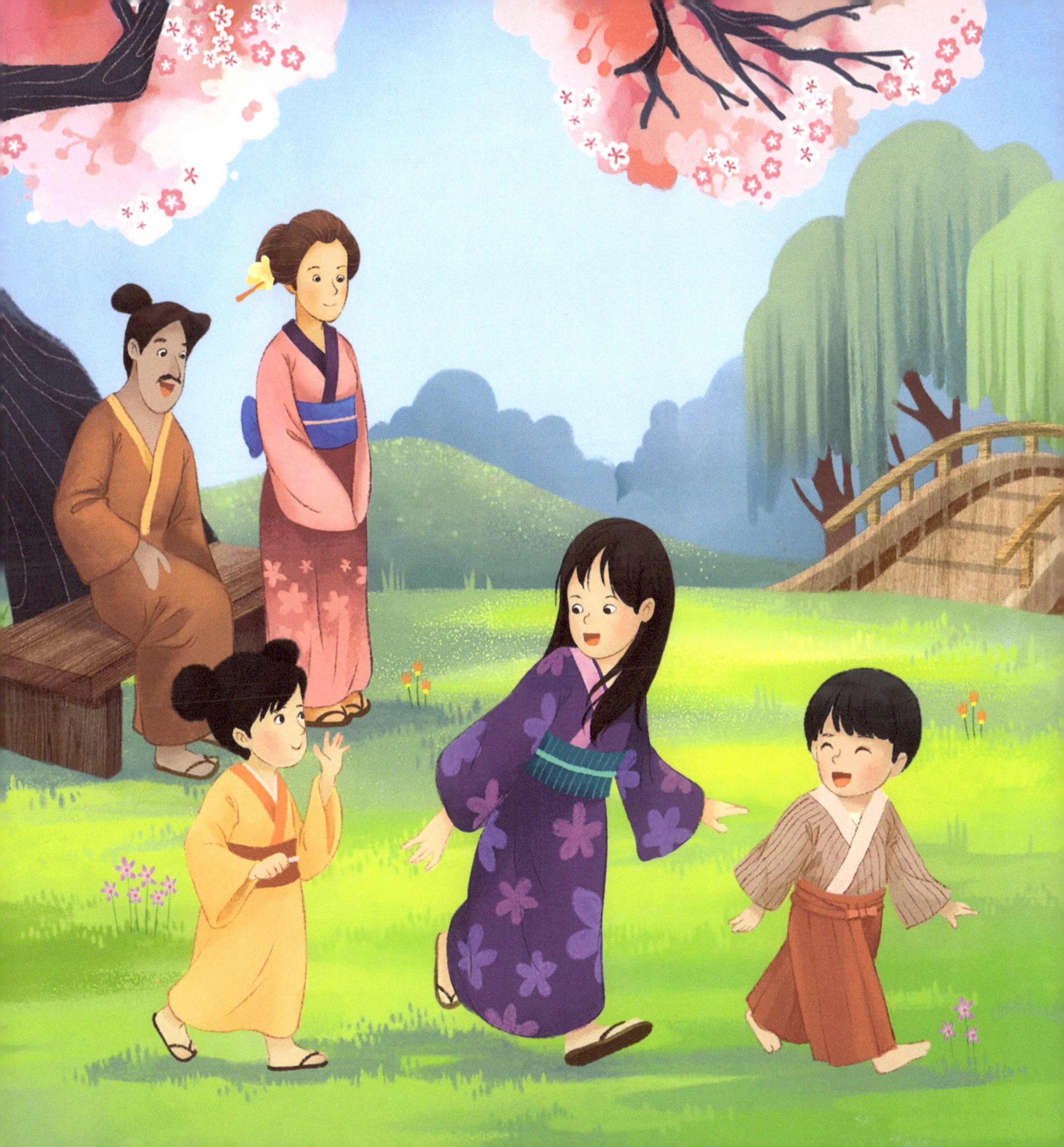

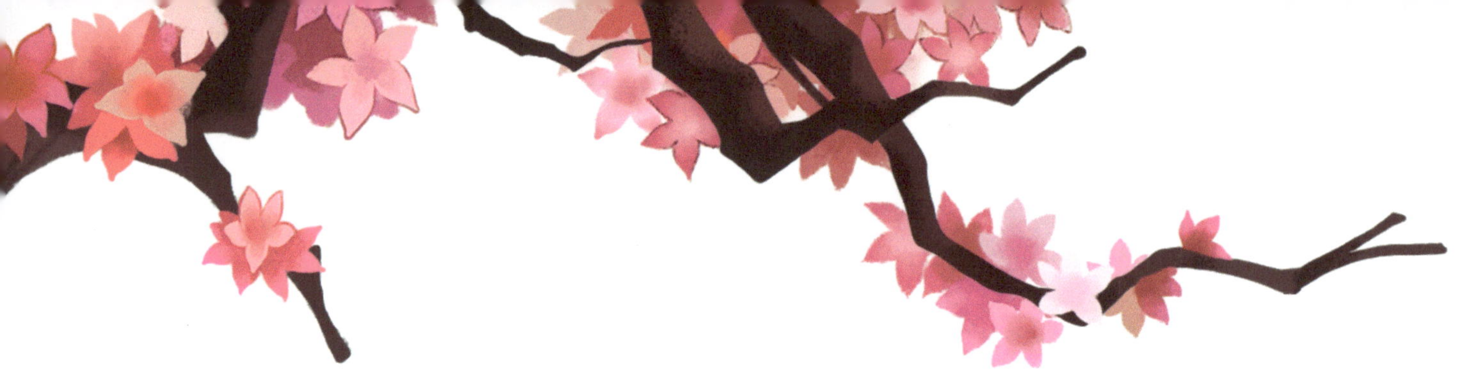

As in all samurai homes, in Takeko's, the
NAGINATA—the samurai weapon—hung on
the wall by the exit of the house.

Every time Takeko went outside, she kept
her eye on the naginata.

She knew it would be hers one day, and
she couldn't wait to grow up and start
training.

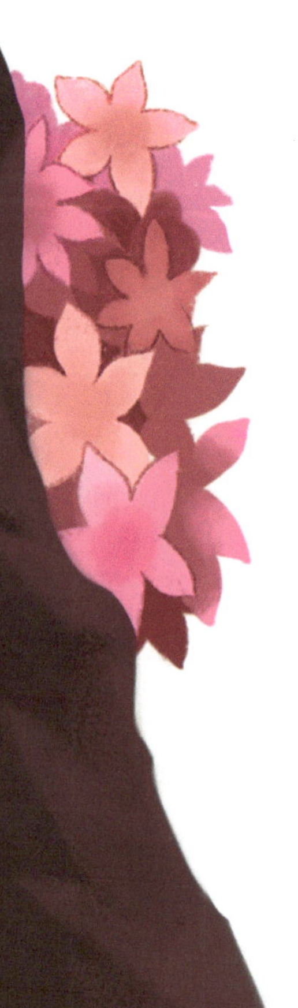

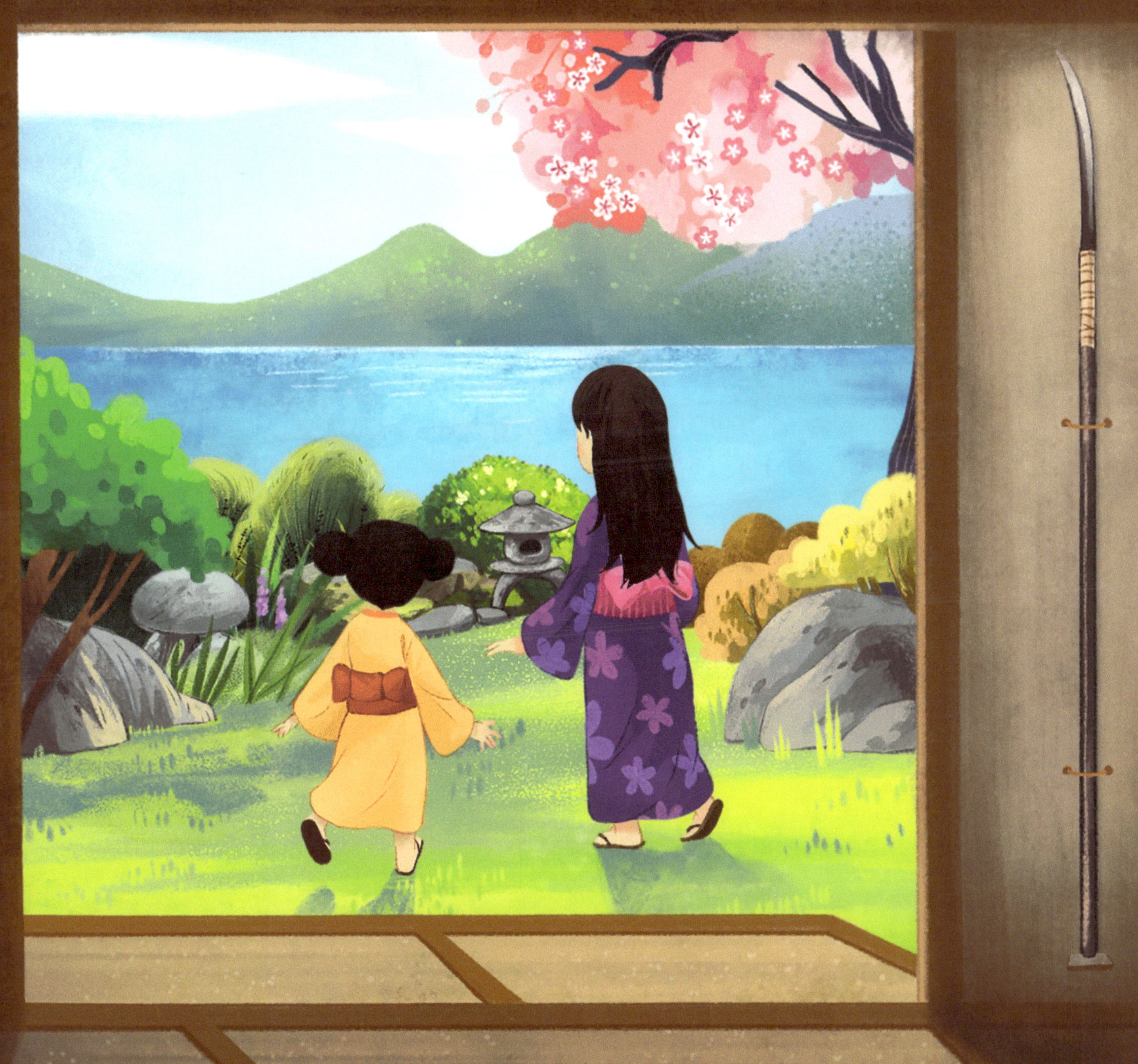

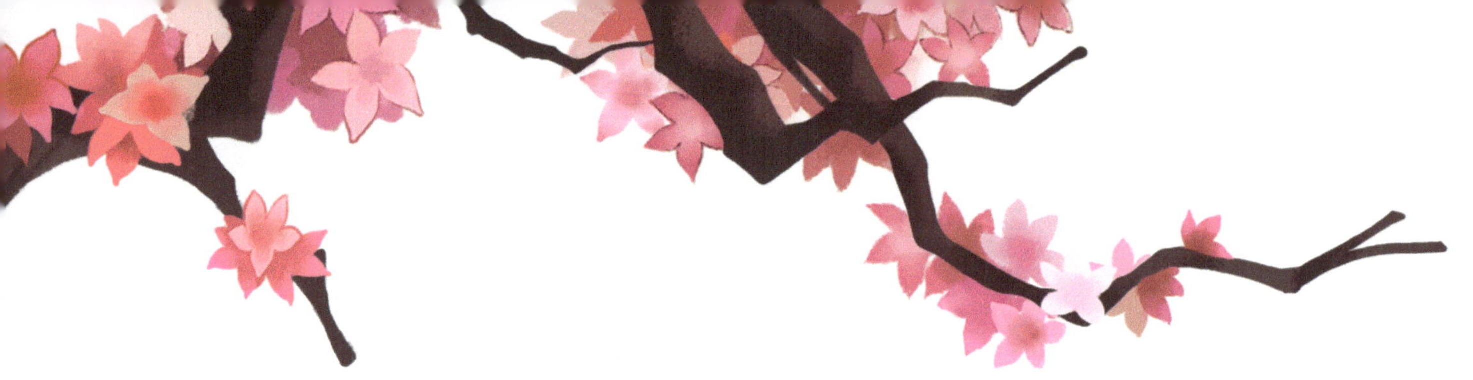

She was quite attached to her mother and especially to her younger sister Yuko.

Yuko often sat and watched Takeko train, looking forward to growing up and following in her sister's footsteps.

Women were also trained to become samurai in the Aizu clan.

Although they were primarily instructed to defend their families, FEMALE SAMURAI were as brave as the male warriors.

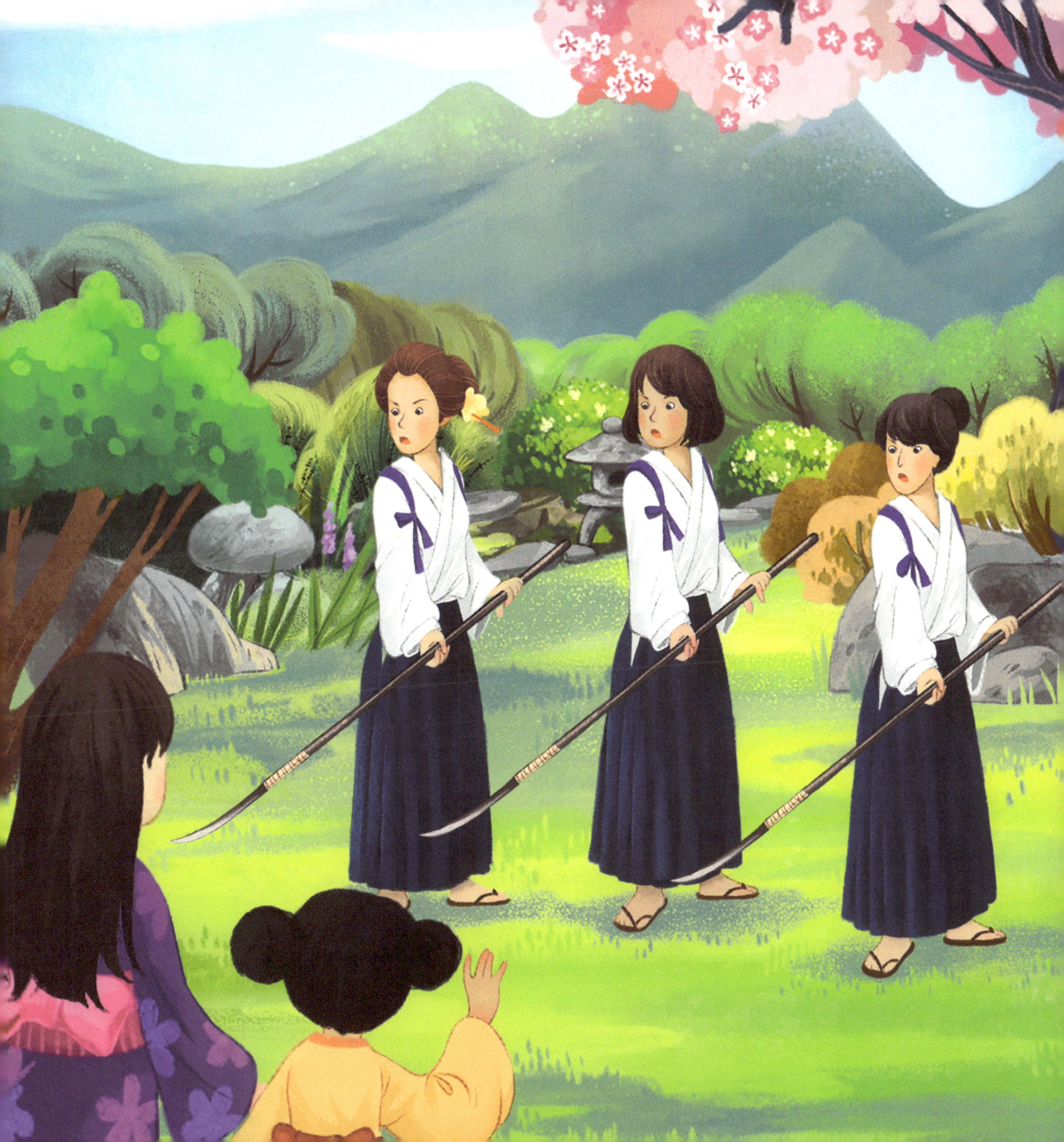

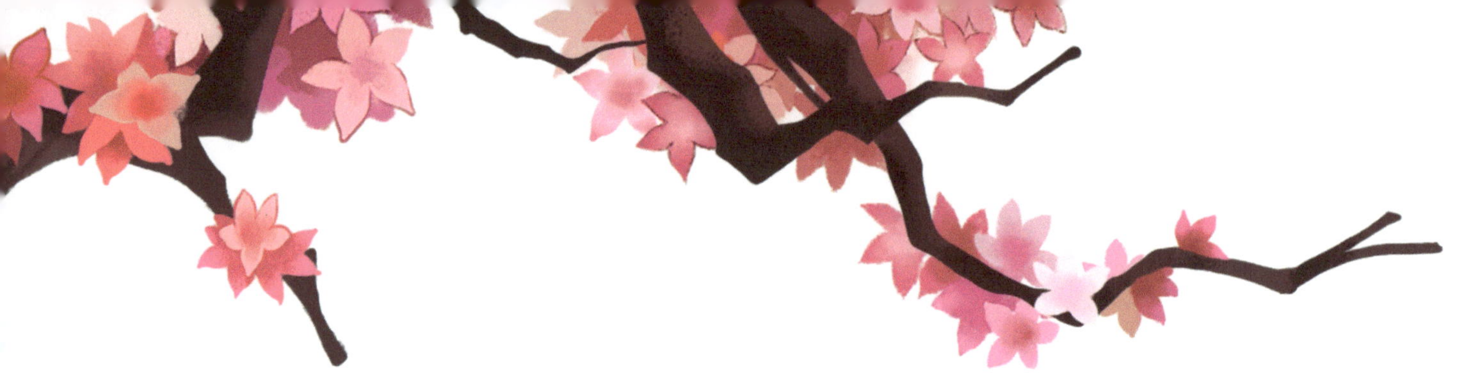

Takeko' family was wealthy, so her parents could afford her the best education.

When Takeko was **SIX YEARS OLD**, her mother took her to the famous master of naginata, Akaoka Daisuke.

Takeko had been eagerly awaiting this moment; she knew she would finally start her naginata training.

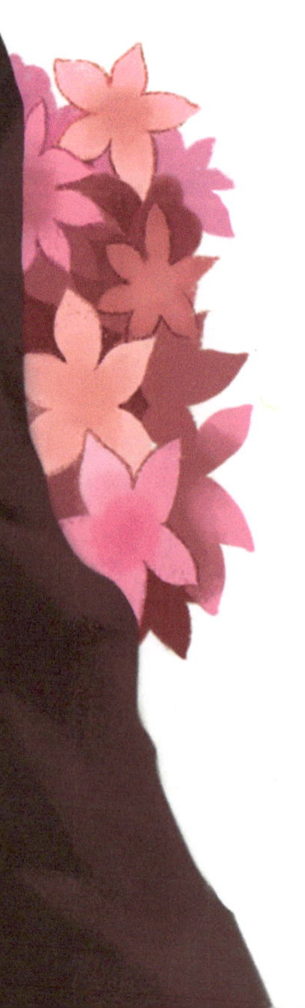

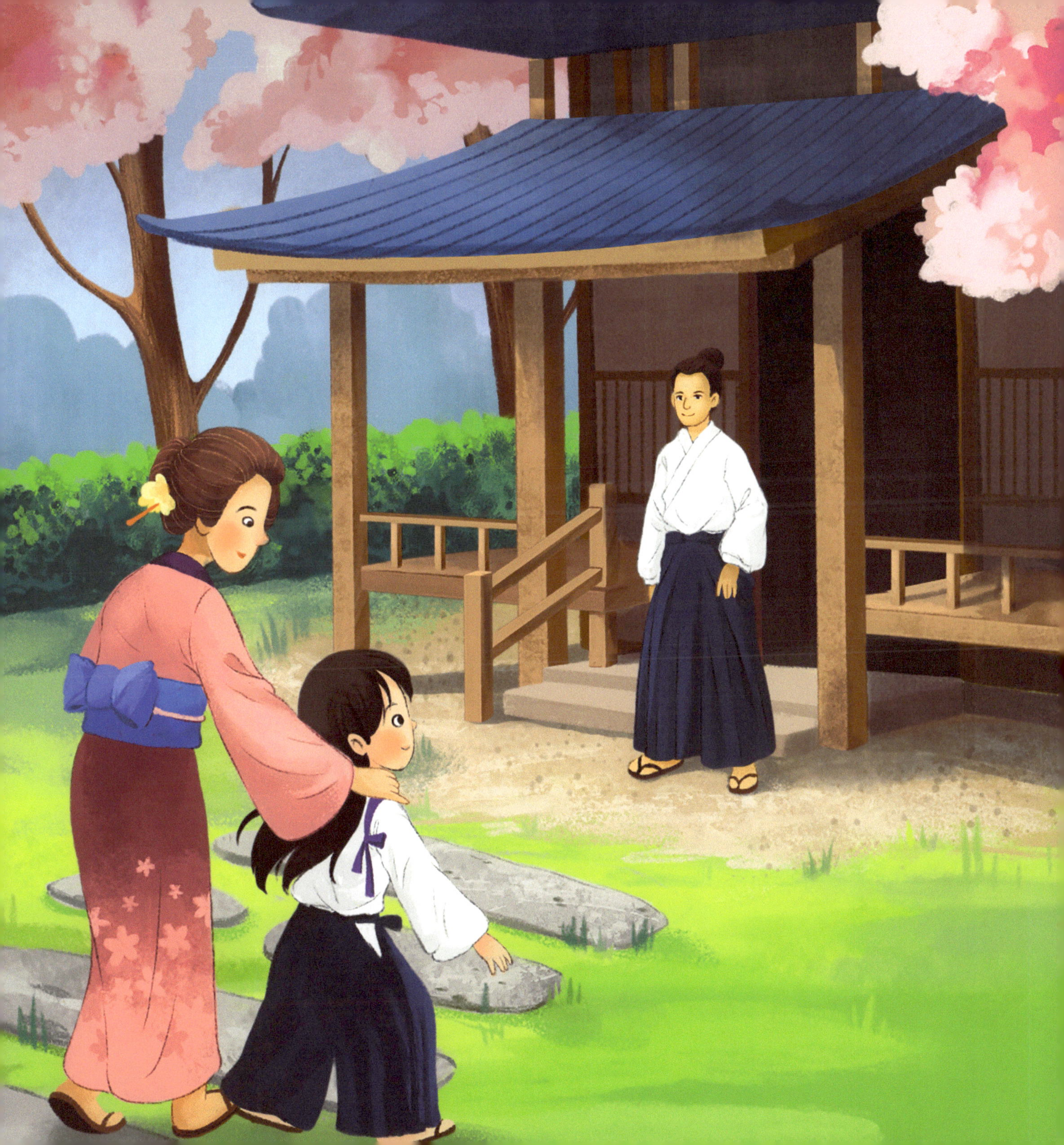

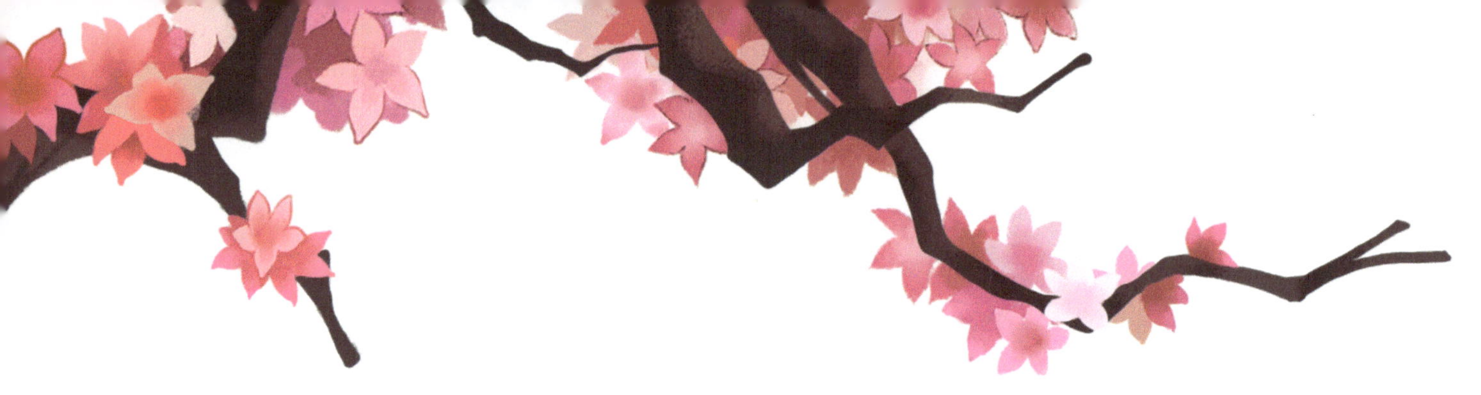

Master Daisuke soon realized that Takeko wasn't an ordinary girl.

She had an unusual talent—not only for martial arts but also for literature and history. Takeko was a HARDWORKING PUPIL and loved learning new things.

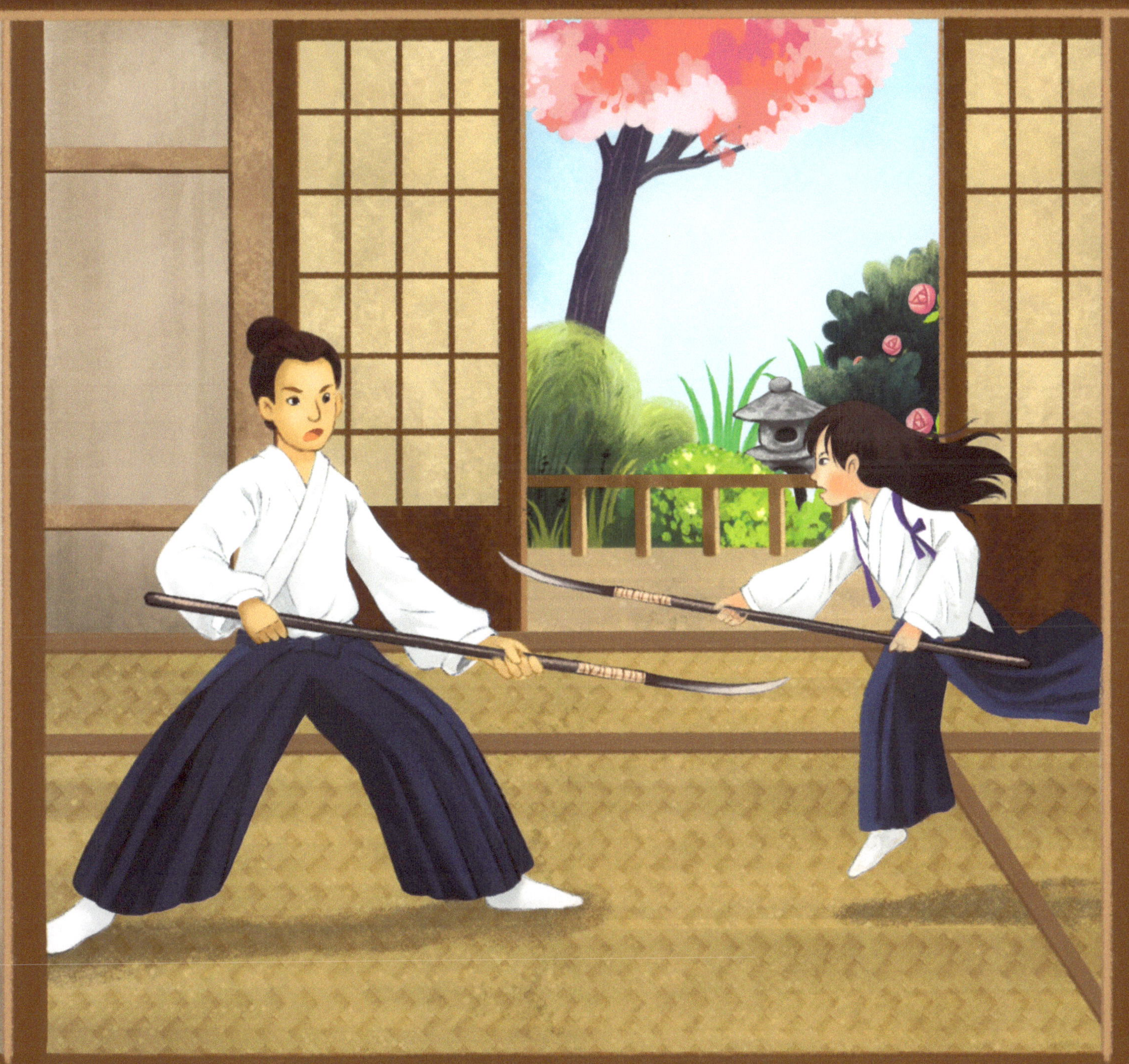

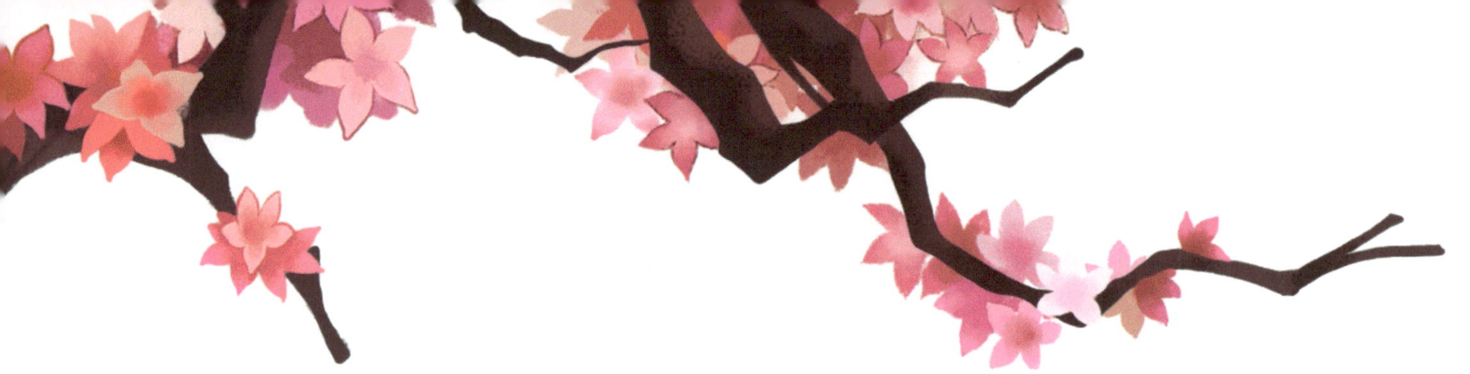

Takeko thrived quickly and achieved excellent results.

She was particularly interested in history and enjoyed reading about Tomoe Gozen, the FEMALE SAMURAI who lived long before her.

Tomoe became her role model; Takeko was inspired by her courage and devotion, aspiring to be just like her.

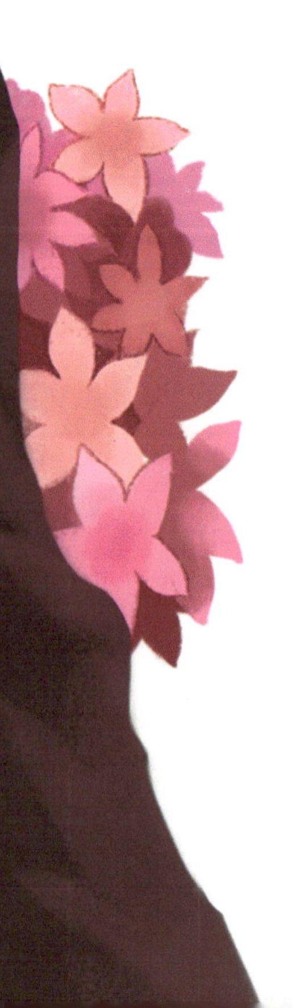

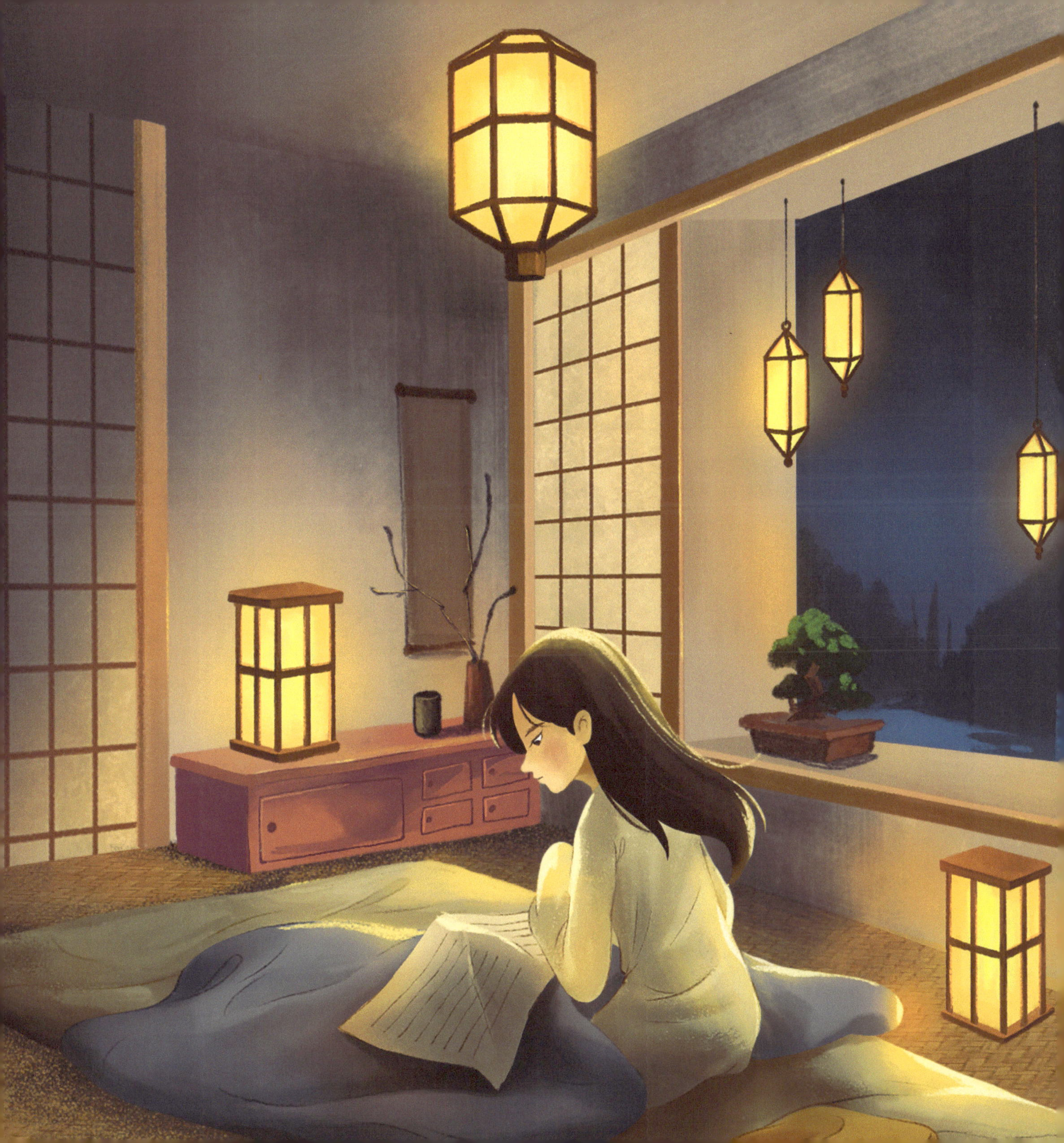

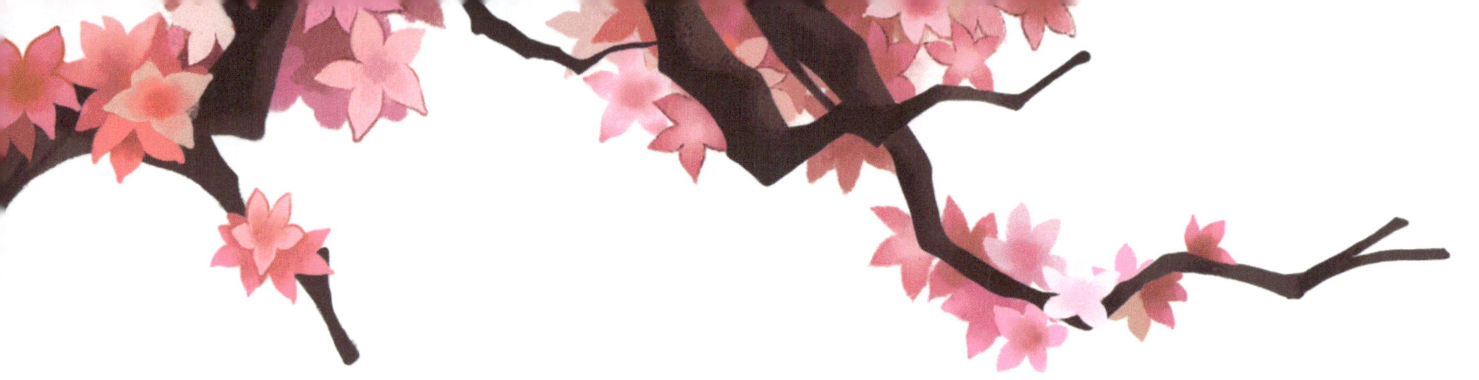

Takeko was so gifted that she became a naginata expert by the time she was sixteen.

Her talent was truly exceptional. During her training, Takeko lived with her teacher, and after several years of hard work, she became the YOUNGEST NAGINATA EXPERT.

When her training was complete, she decided to return to her family.

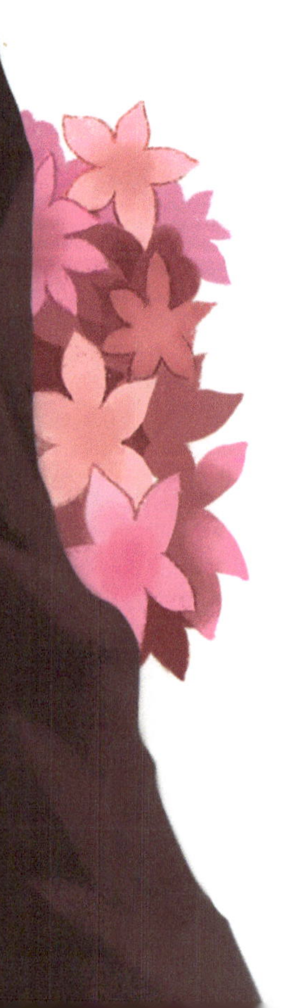

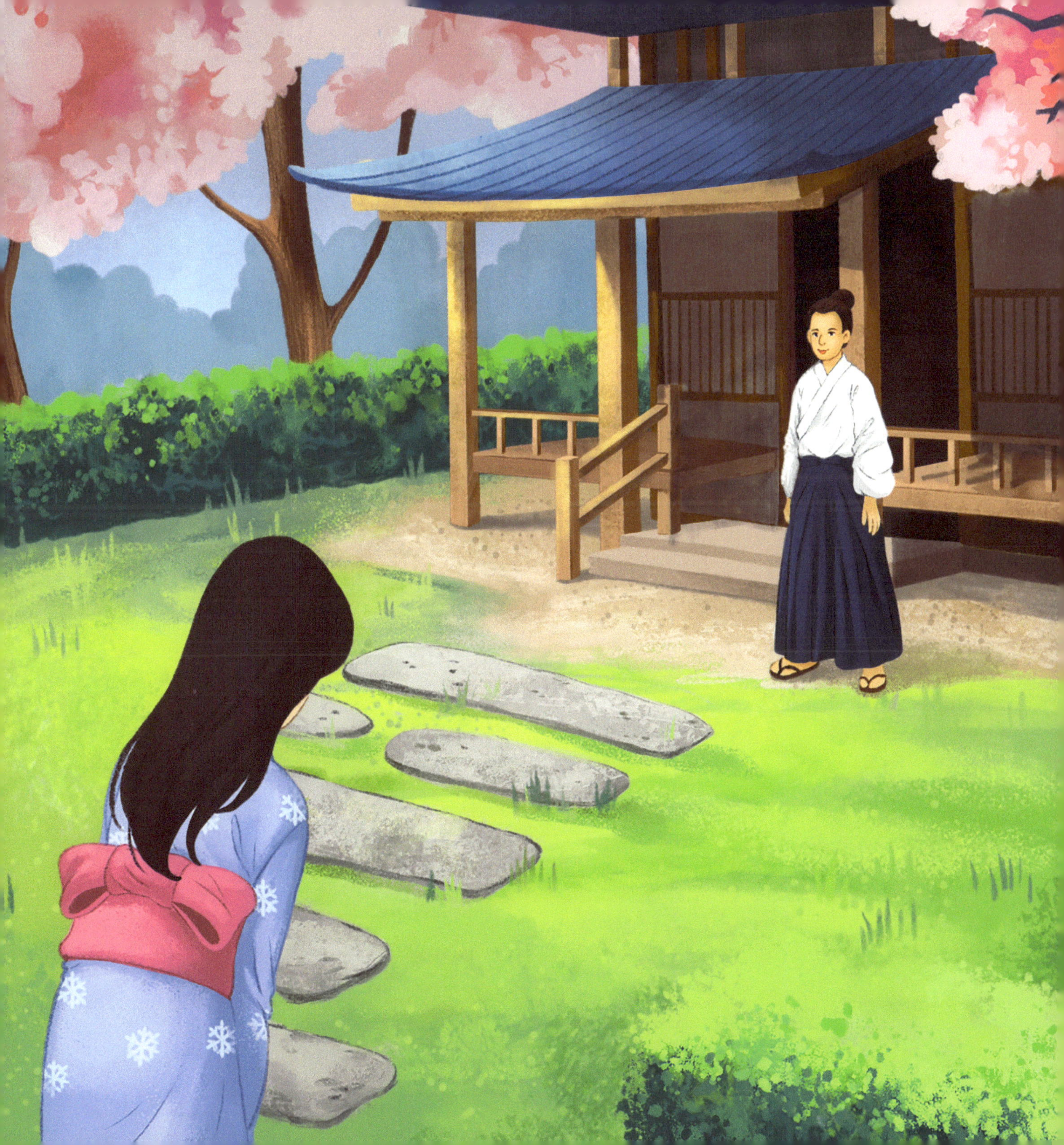

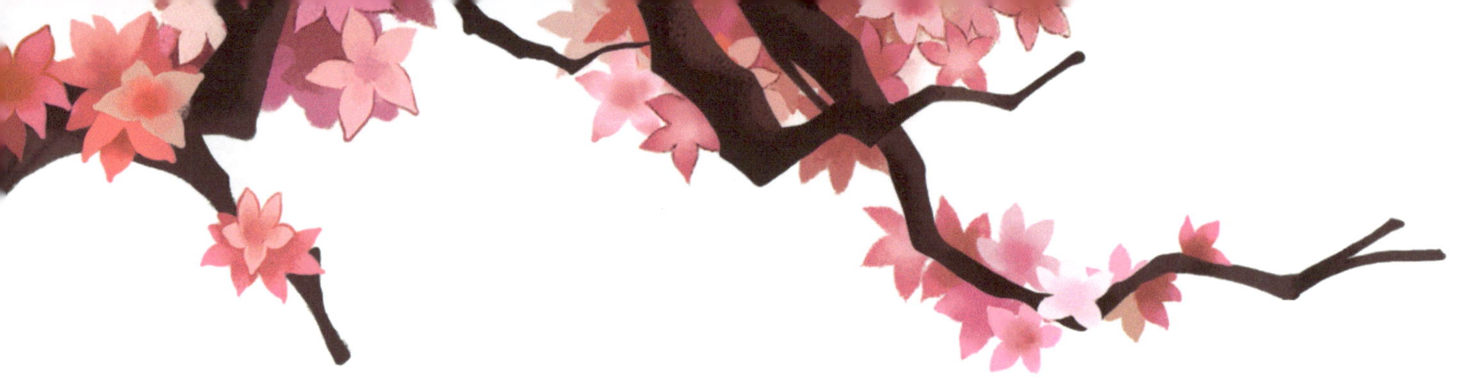

At that time, Japan was undergoing significant changes—changes that would alter the nation and the fate of its inhabitants forever.

Takeko closely monitored the situation in the country, where war was looming.

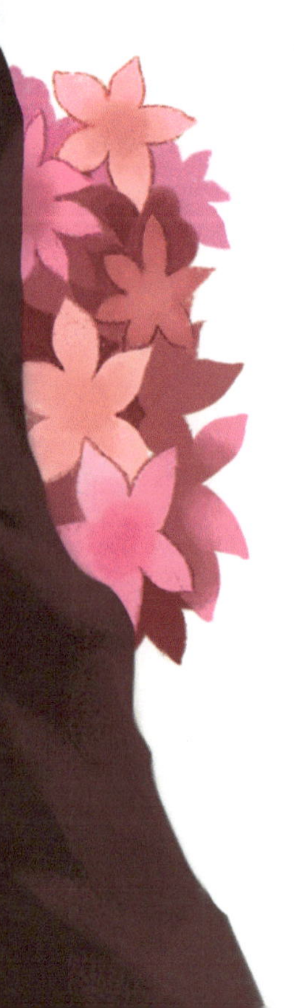

Soon, **CONFLICT ERUPTED** between the Imperial Army and the Shogunate.

Loyal to the Shogun and the Aizu clan, Takeko joined the fight on their side.

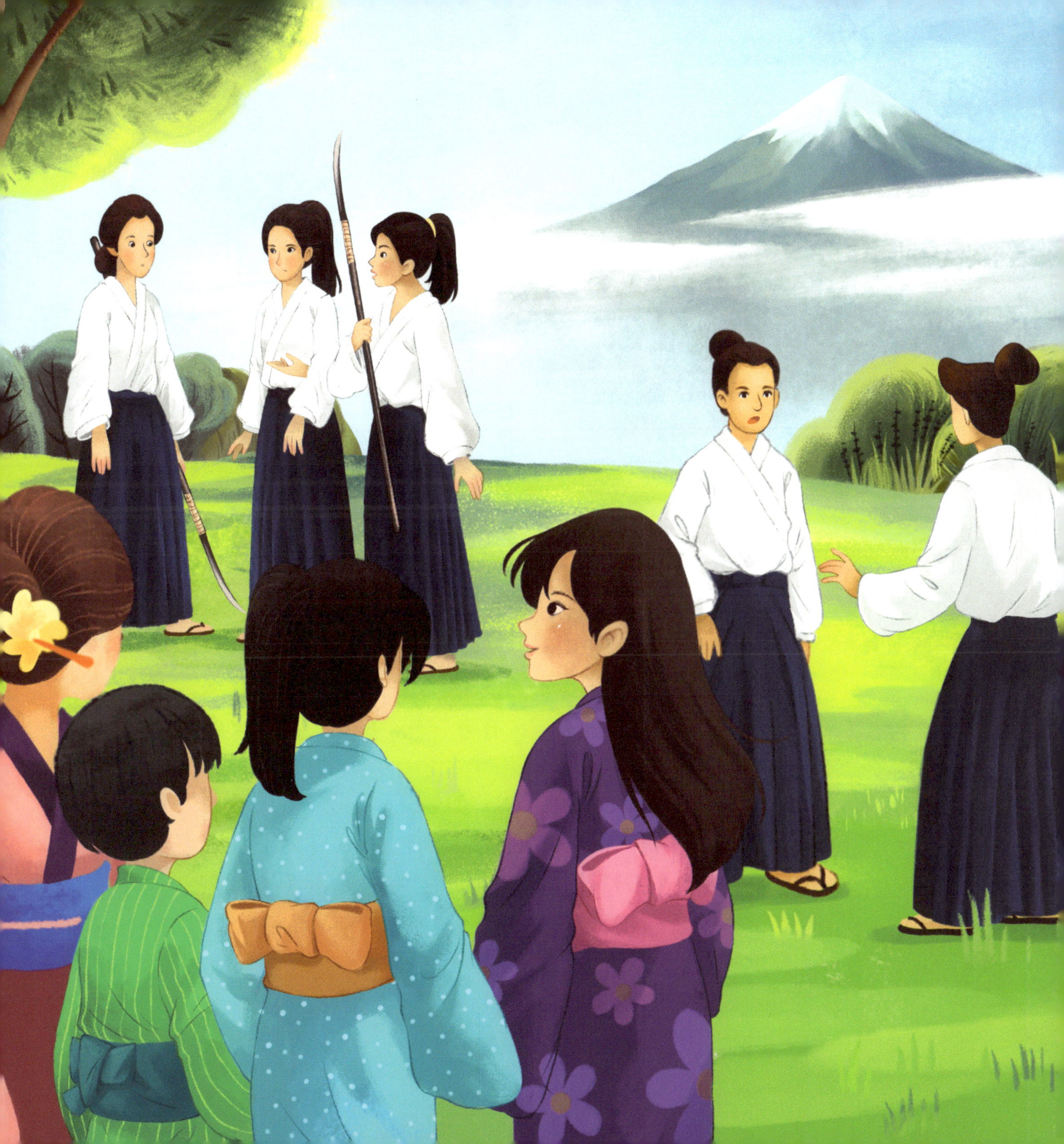

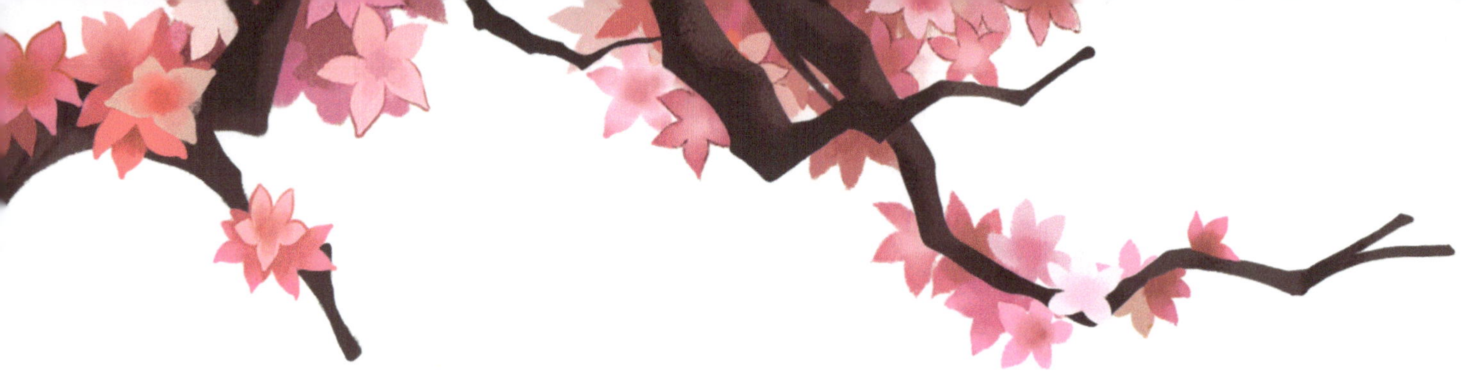

The night before her first battle, Takeko and her mother debated what to do with Yuko.

They worried for her safety because she was so young.

They hesitated over whether to take her with them or leave her behind.

In the end, they decided to bring her along. It was a difficult decision.

That night, Takeko wrote on a piece of paper, which she attached to her naginata:

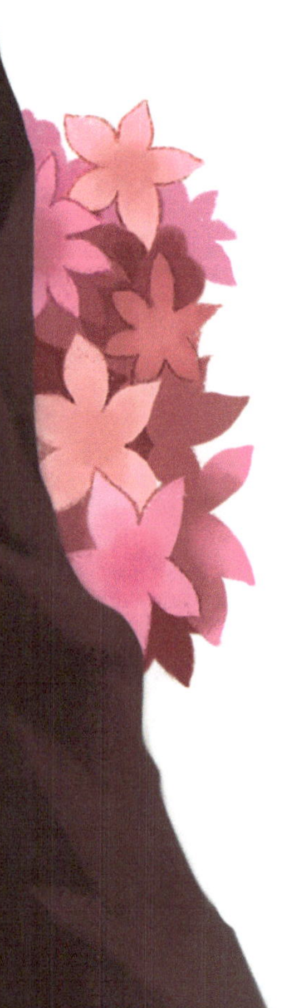

"I WOULD NOT DARE TO COUNT MYSELF AMONG THE FAMOUS WARRIORS—EVEN THOUGH I SHARE THE SAME BRAVE HEART."

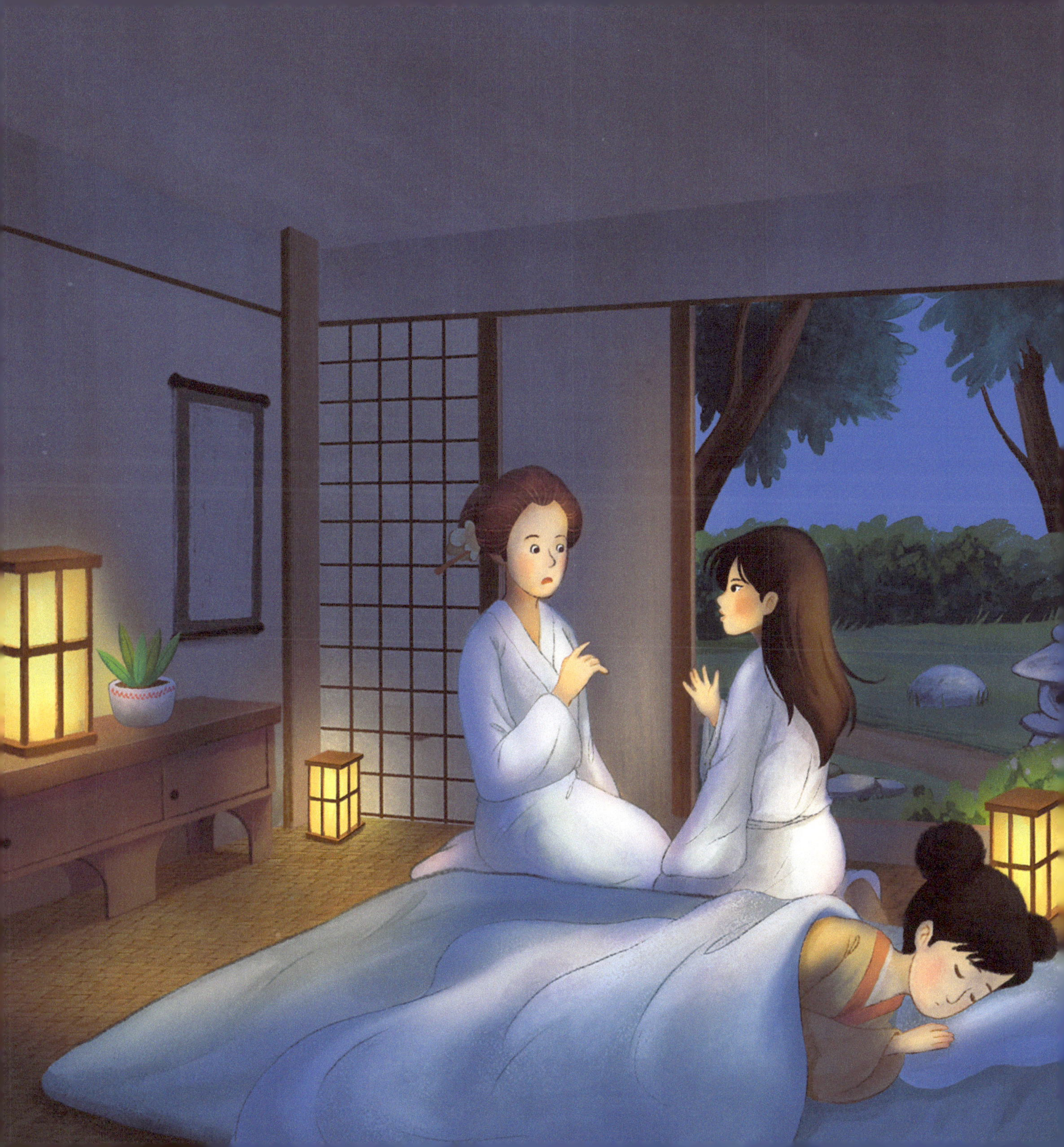

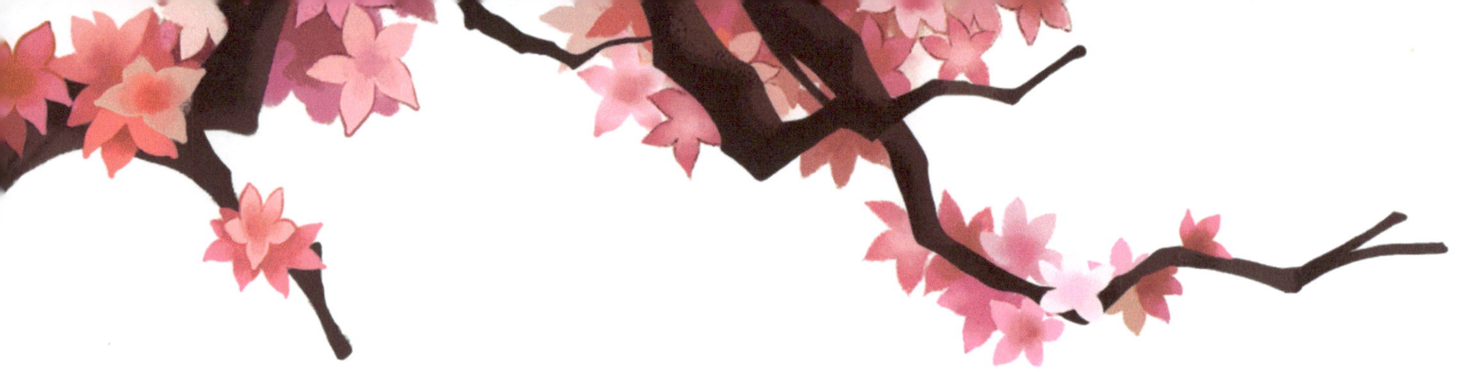

Together with her mother, sister, and other warriors, Takeko joined the samurai army.

Although women were just as brave and as well-trained as the male samurai, they weren't allowed to fight alongside them in the Aizu clan.

Her brother Toyonori left with their father.

Takeko was resolved to fight. She wanted to defend her clan—she had trained her whole life for it. Although she knew that women were not permitted to battle alongside the male samurai, she was DETERMINED to change that.

She visited the Army commander and informed him that she and her fellow warriors would not back down.

Her persistence finally paid off, and they were allowed to fight alongside the male samurai.

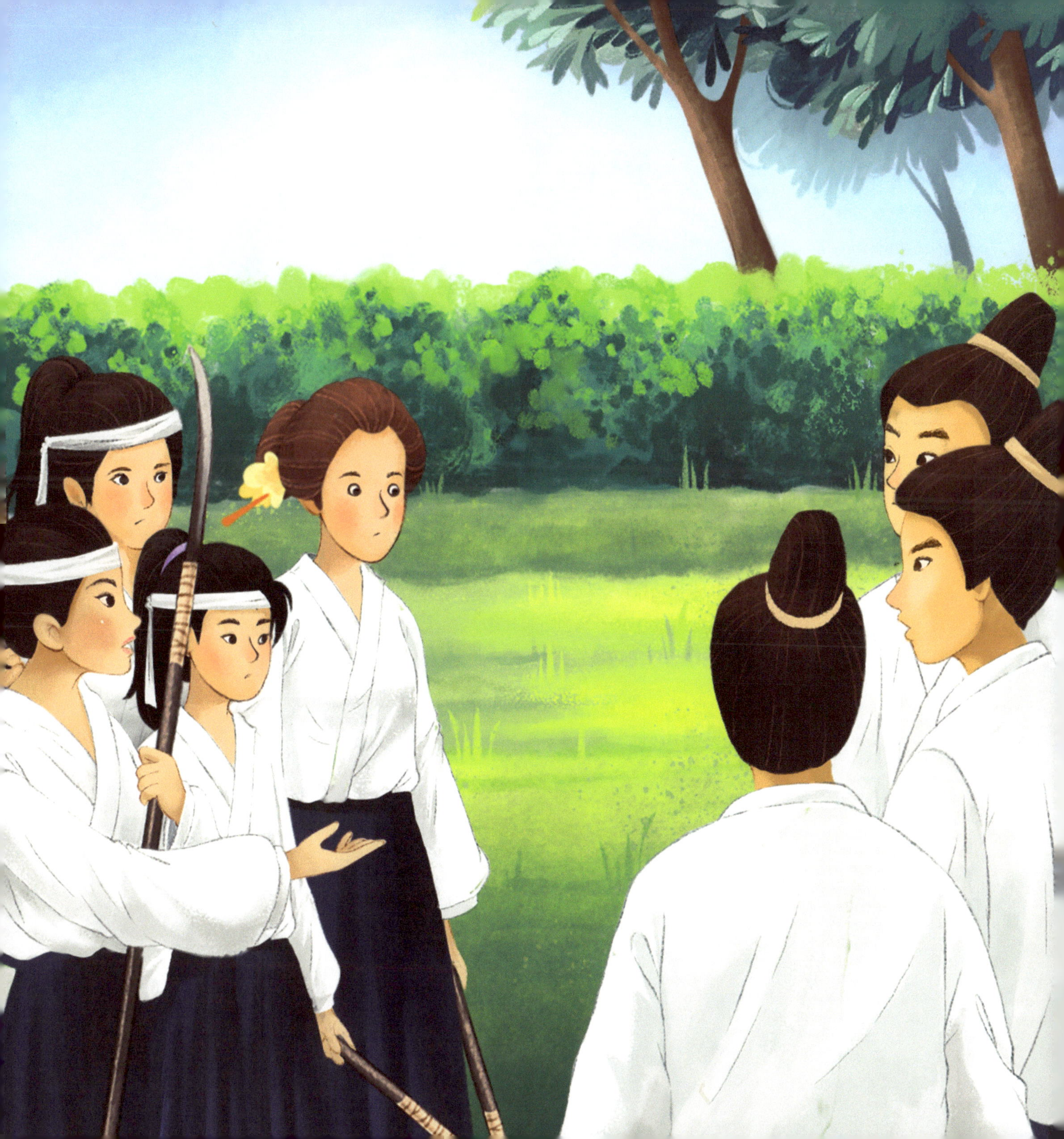

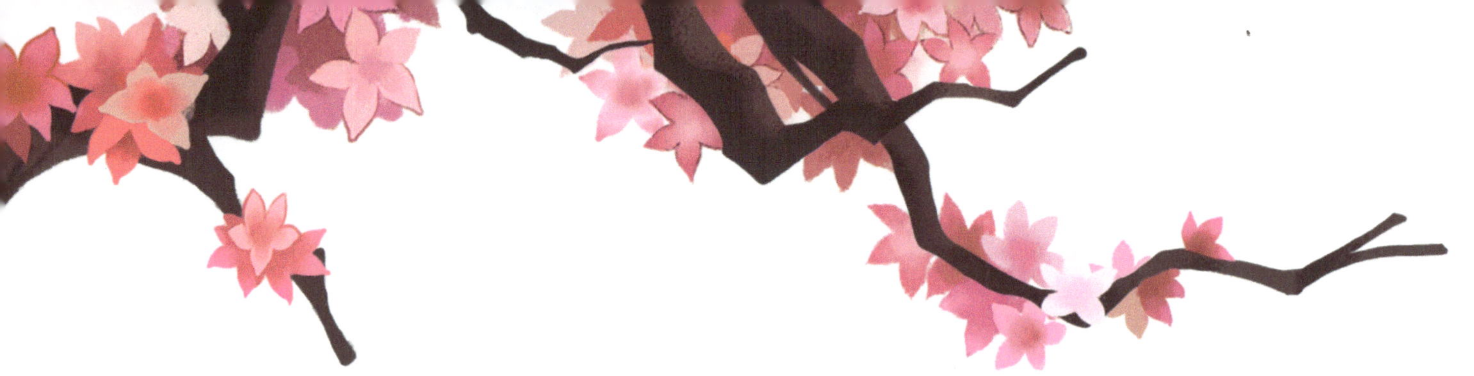

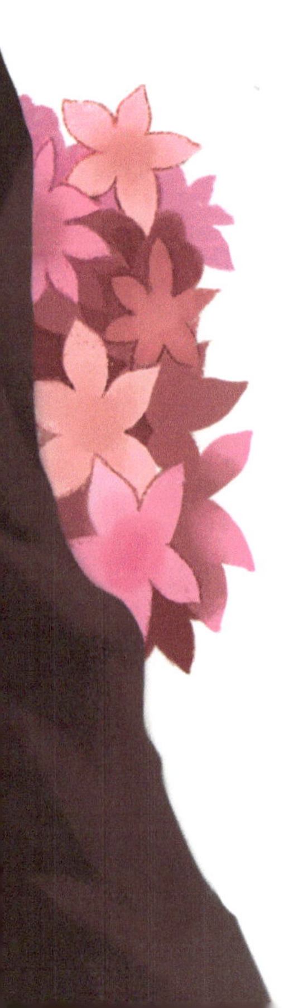

That morning, in front of Wakamatsu Castle, Takeko and her fellow female warriors stood side by side with the male samurai as the fighting began.

The Aizu clan fought against the numerous and better-armed Imperial Army.

Takeko fought bravely, like a LIONESS, defeating many samurai, and her skills were soon recognized.

During the battle, they moved closer and closer to the Yanagi Bridge.

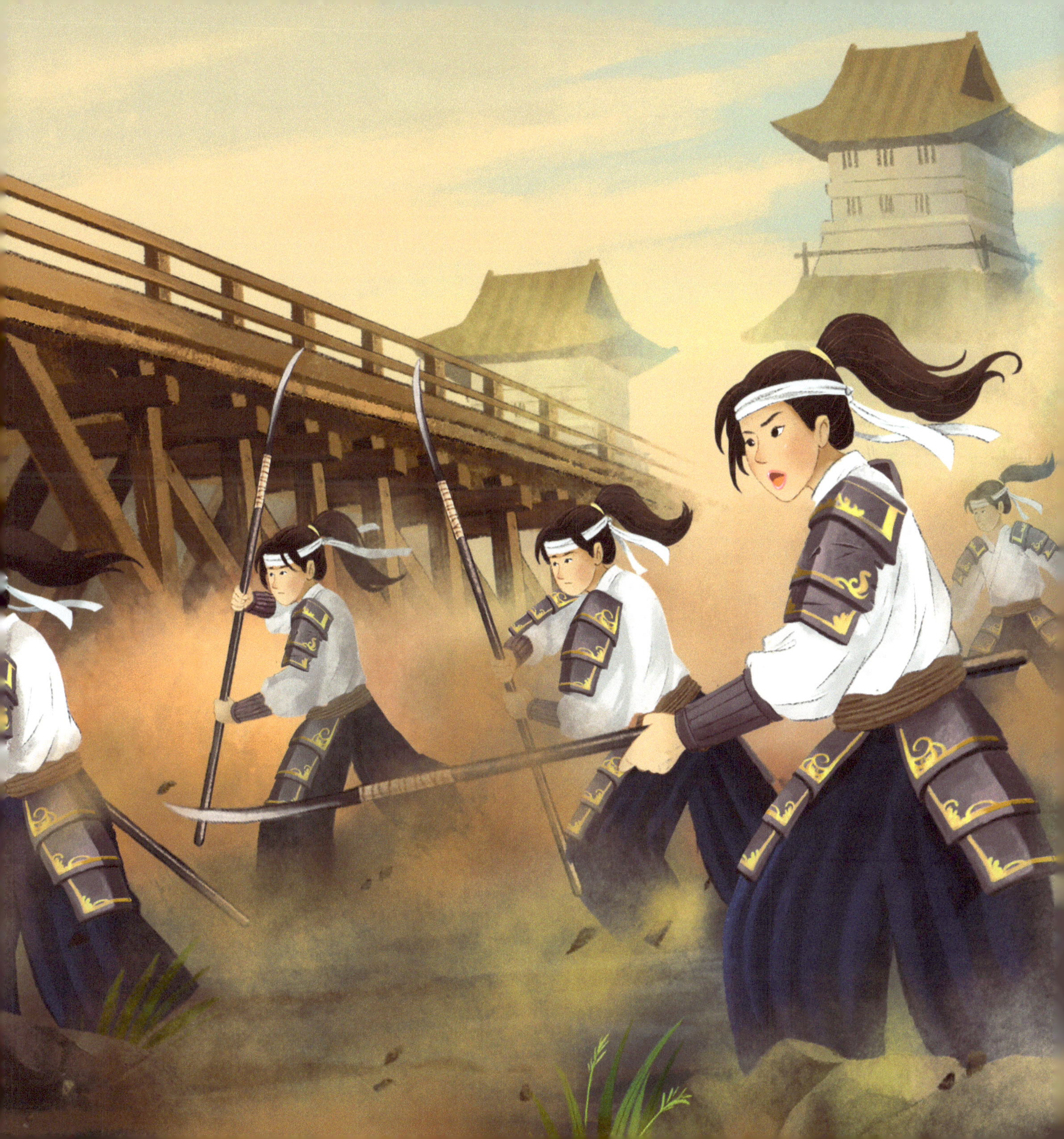

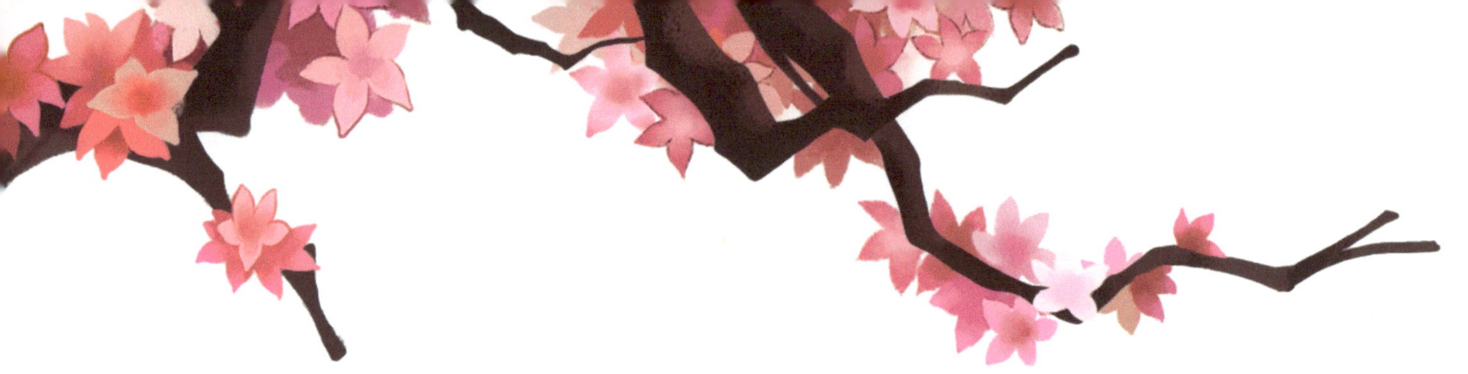

Unfortunately, some soldiers in the Imperial Army carried firearms.

One soldier, who saw Takeko fighting, fired a bullet in her direction and struck her in the chest.

Takeko did not survive.

Yuko RUSHED to her dying sister to help, but there was nothing she could do.

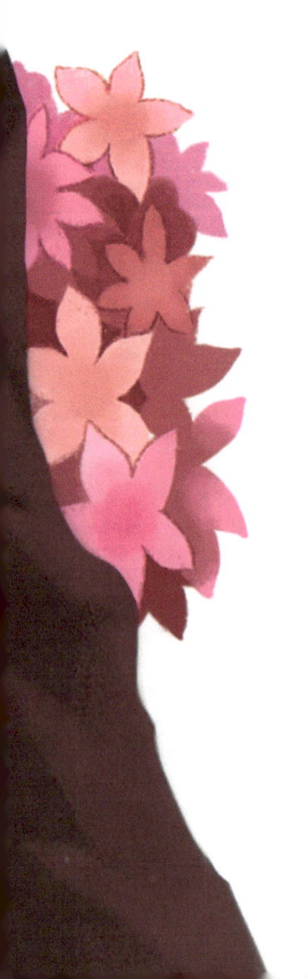

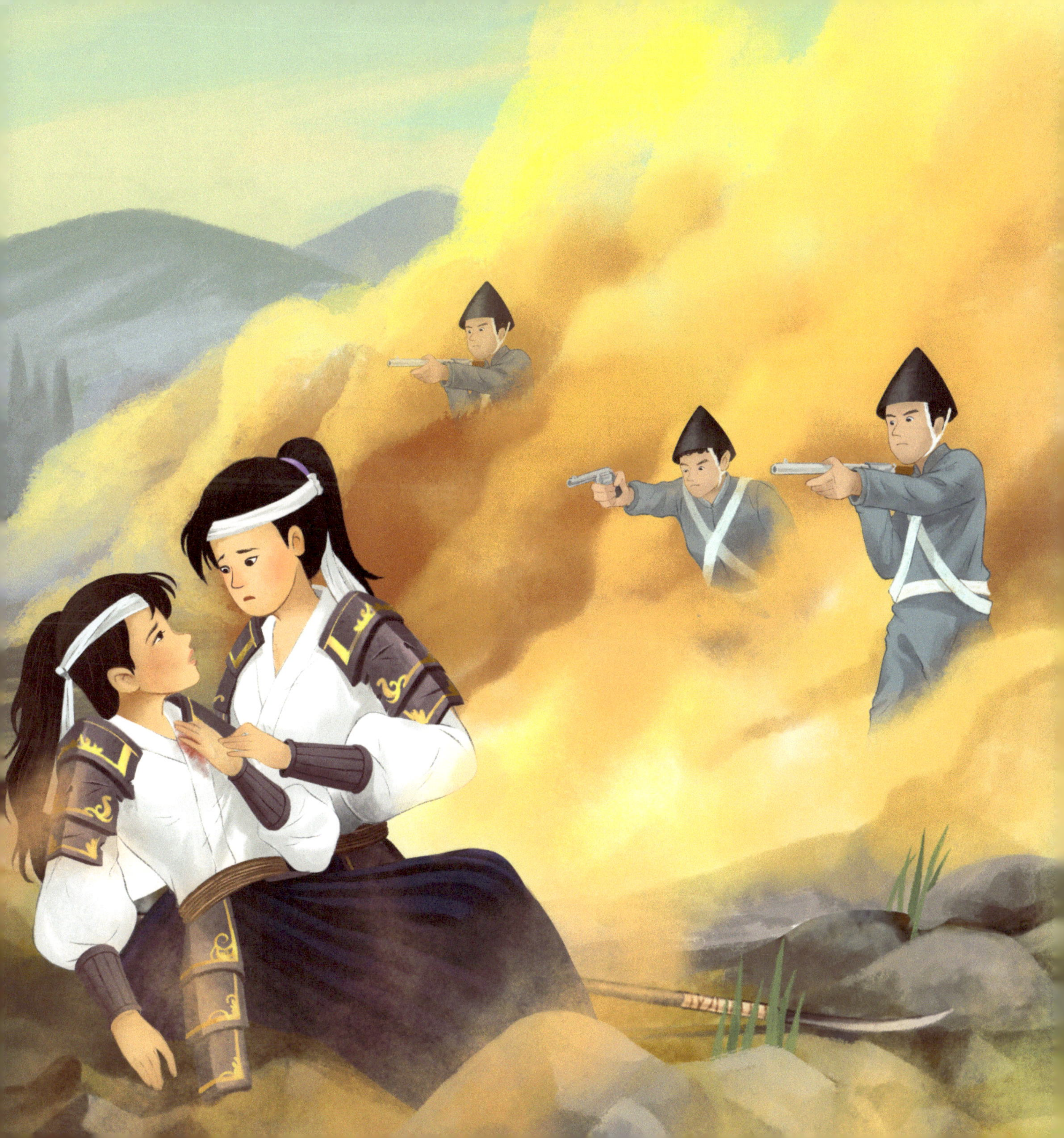

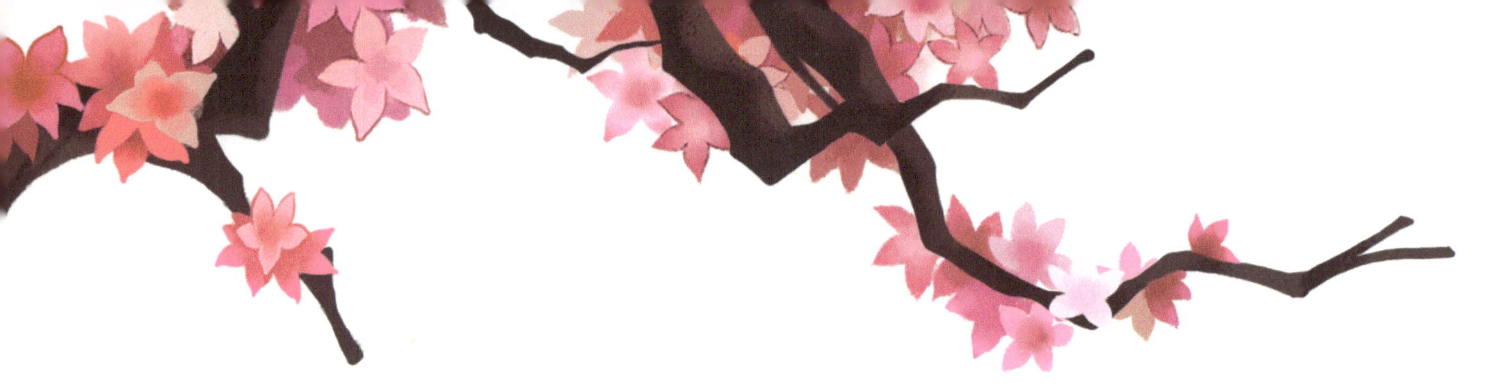

They managed to carry Takeko's lifeless body to HOKAI TEMPLE, where she was buried under a pine tree where she remains to this day.

Her naginata was donated to the temple.

All the members of Takeko's family survived the war, except for her.

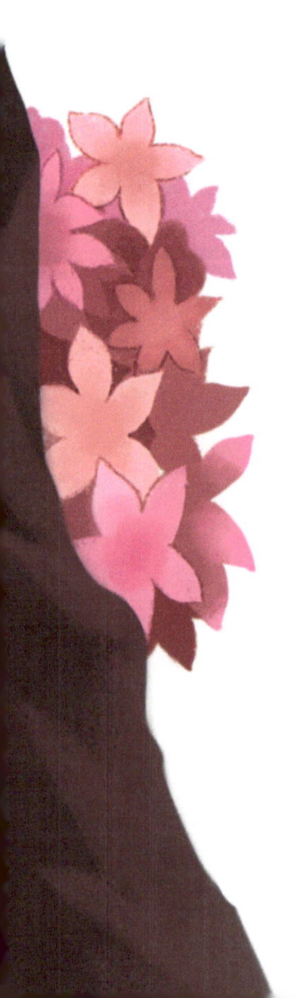

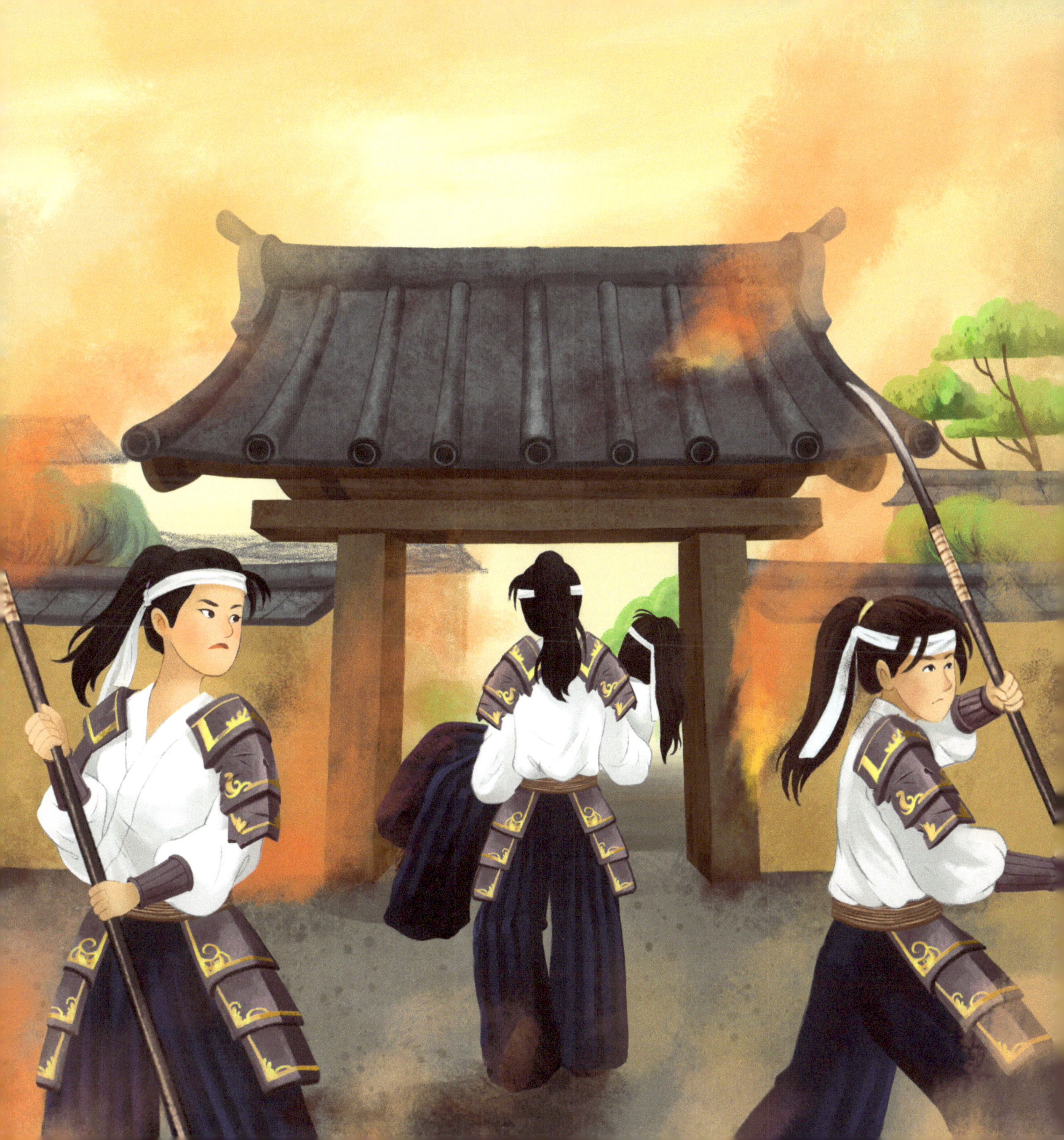

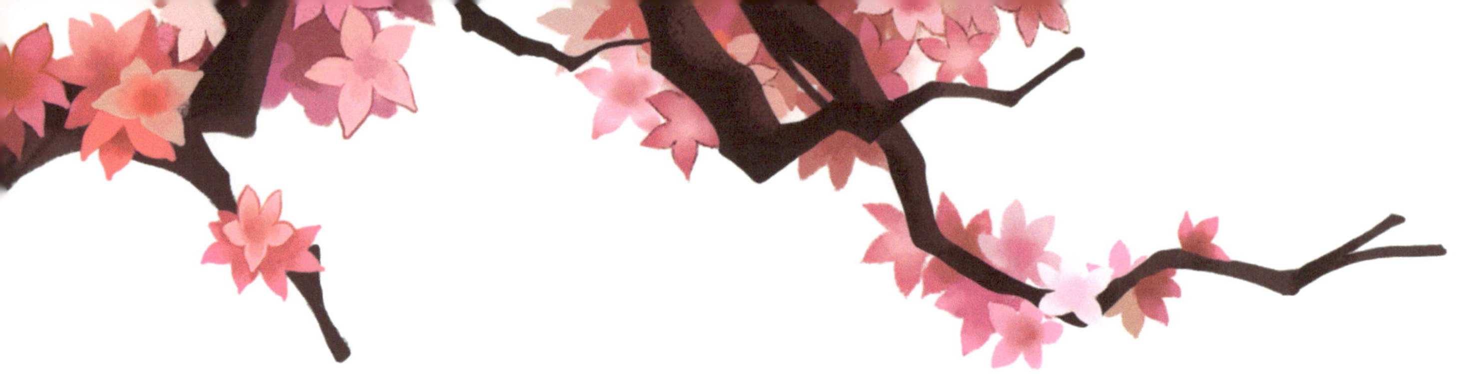

With Takeko's death, the era of the samurai came to an end.

It marked the end of the Shogunate, the samurai, and a **LONG PERIOD** of conflict.

Her statue stands proudly in the Hōkai-ji Temple Park, serving as a lasting reminder of her unwavering loyalty and remarkable courage.

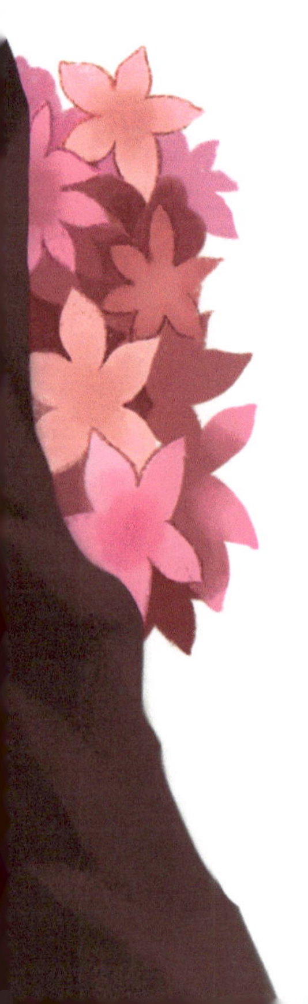

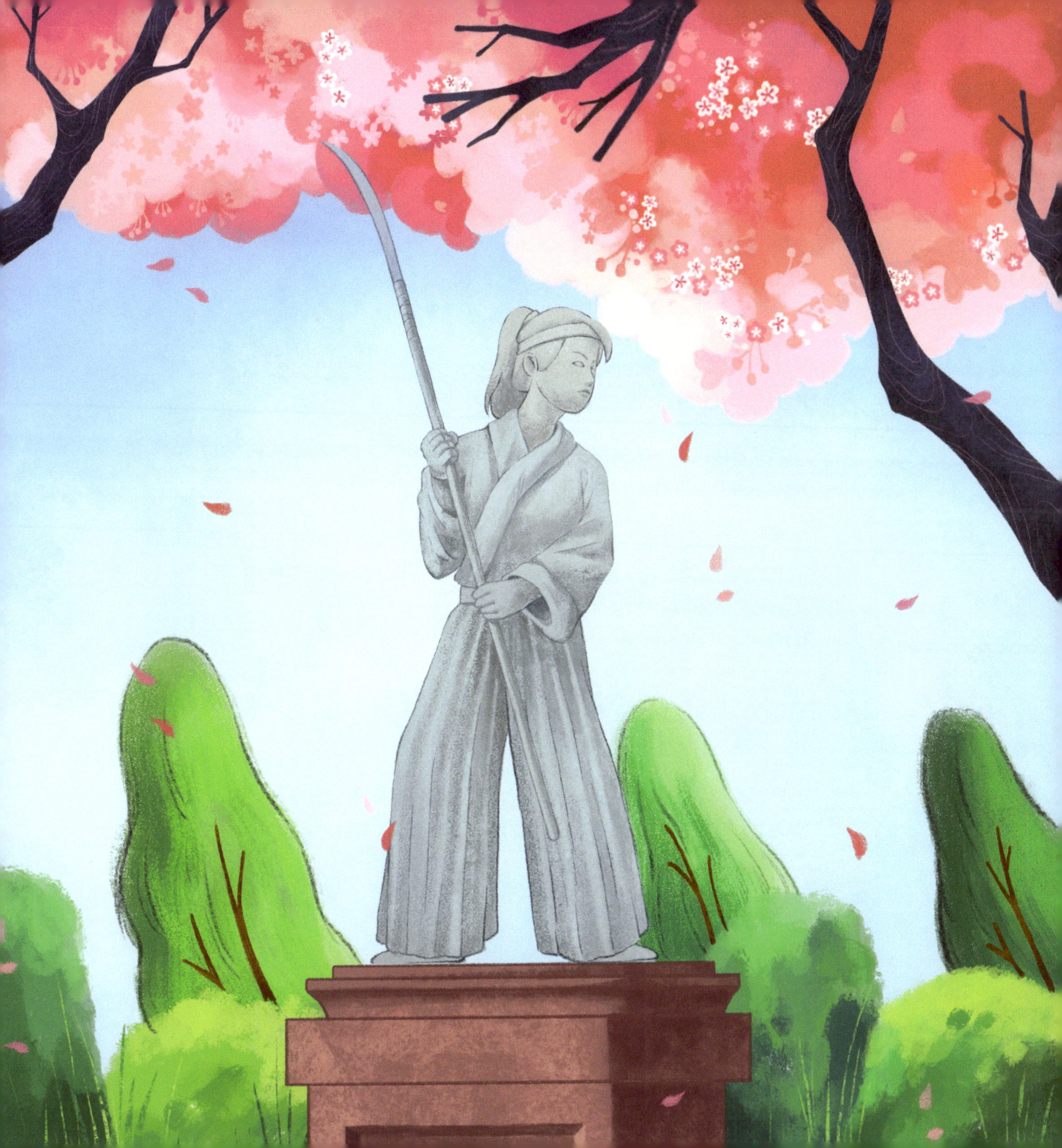

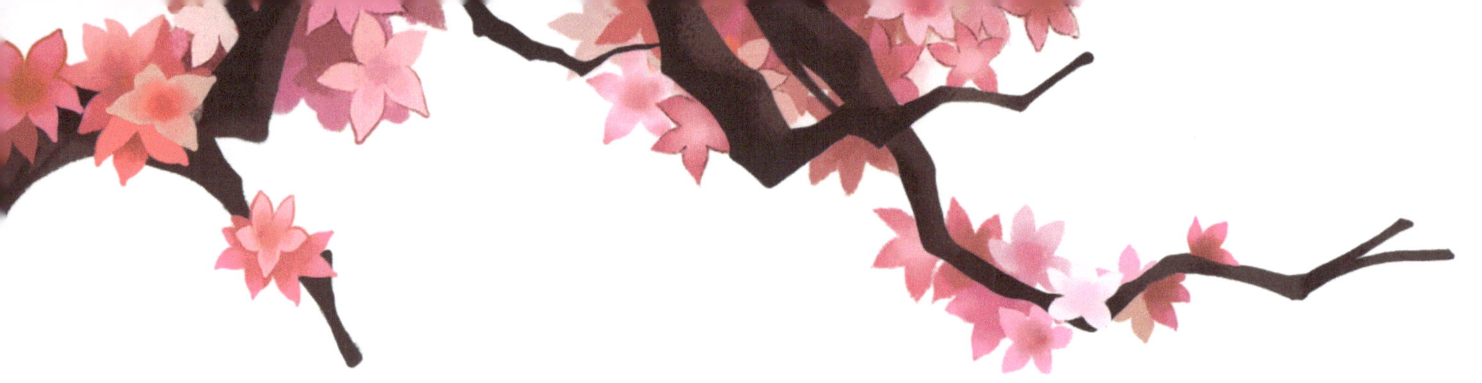

Although Takeko lost her life at such a young age, she will never be forgotten.

She remains one of the most prominent and bravest women in Japan's history.

Every autumn, in her honor, a festival is held where girls with white bands on their heads march and pay tribute to Takeko and her fellow warriors.

TAKEKO LIVES ON IN THE HEARTS AND MINDS OF THE JAPANESE PEOPLE.

She continues to be a role model for many girls, who training naginata as a sport today.

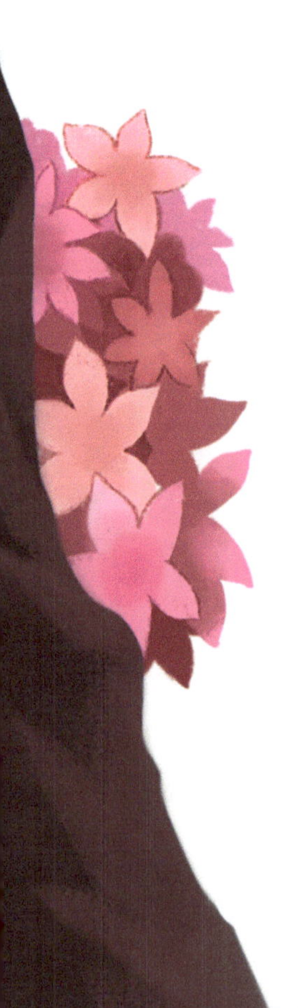

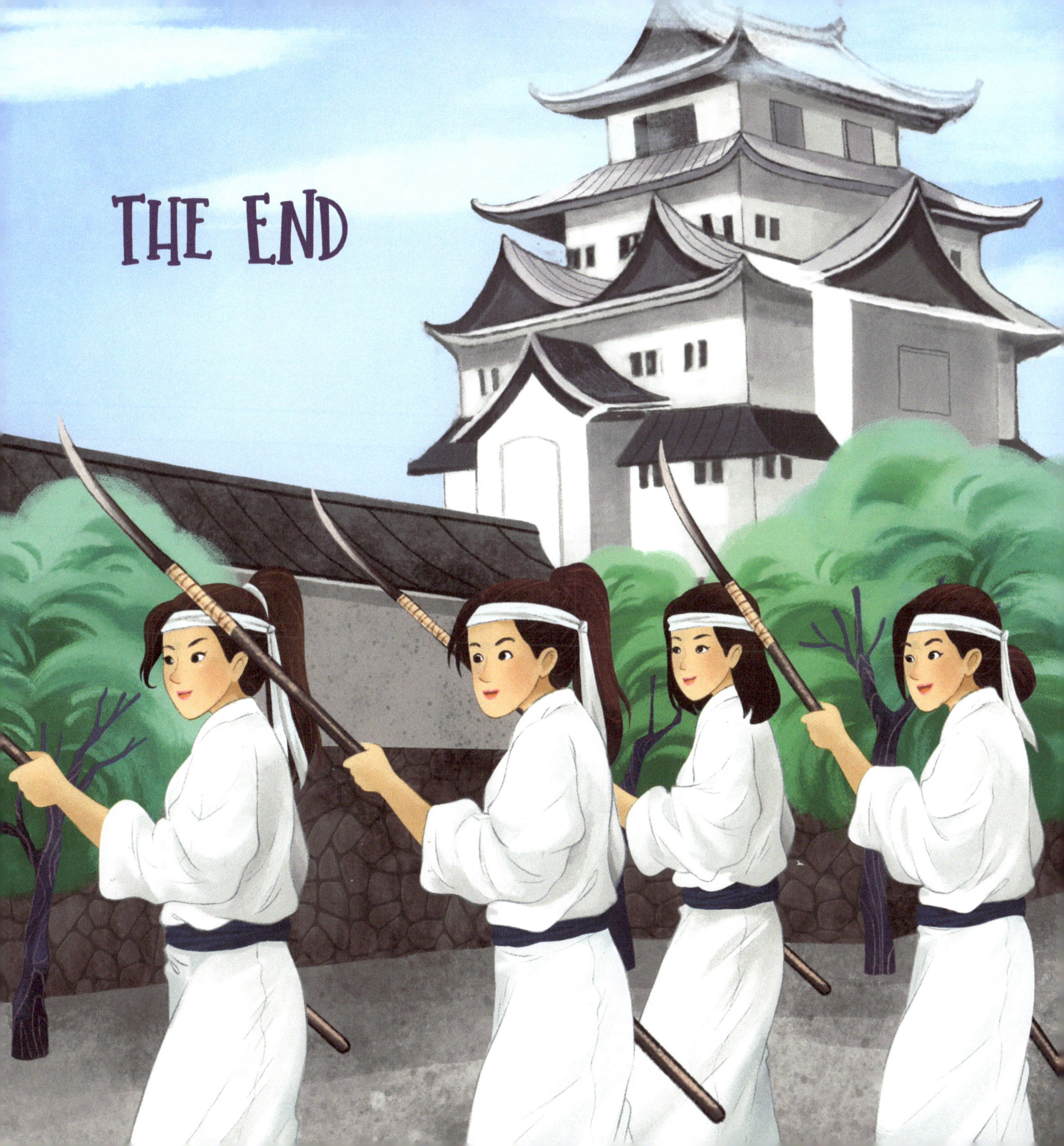
THE END

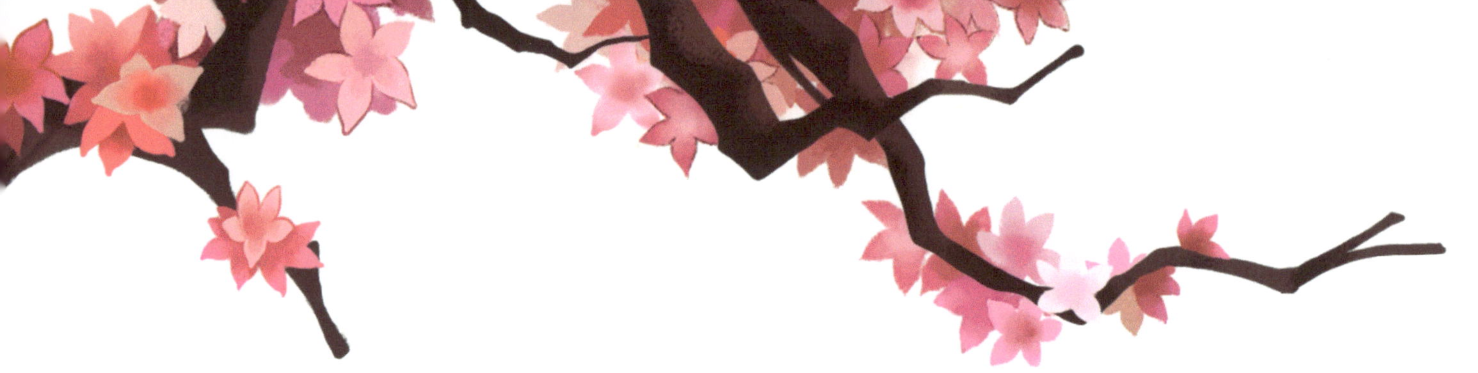

GLOSSARY

- Edo: Tokyo today

- Aizu : A region in Japan

- Samurai: Members of the warrior class in Japan

- Shogun: A powerful military leader in Japan

- Naginata: A traditional Japanese weapon with a long pole and a curved blade

- Martial Arts: Special types of training that teach people how to defend themselves, fight, and stay healthy

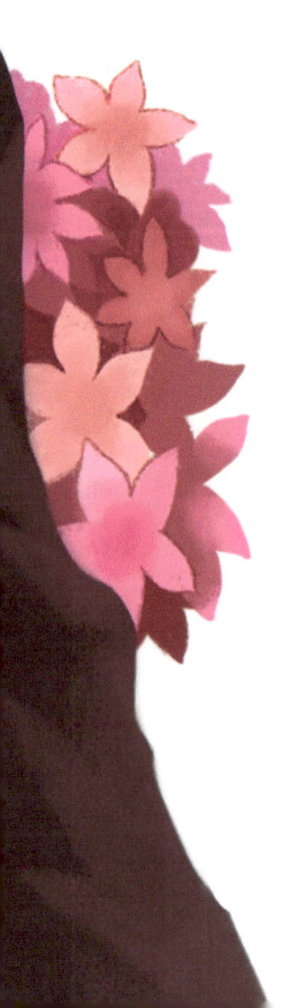

TAKEKO'S WARRIORS

The Joshitai (娘子隊) was a group of female warriors formed during the Boshin War in Japan, which took place from 1868 to 1869. This group was unique because it was made up of women, a rarity in the predominantly male samurai tradition. Led by Nakano Takeko, the Joshitai fought courageously for the Aizu Domain in northern Japan against the forces of the newly established Meiji government.

The women of the Joshitai were not officially part of the Aizu army; they formed their own unit voluntarily. They armed themselves primarily with traditional weapons like naginata (a type of pole weapon) and were motivated by a strong sense of loyalty and honor toward their families and their homeland. Nakano Takeko, a highly skilled martial artist and a respected samurai, became the leader of this small but determined force.

The most famous battle involving the Joshitai was the Battle of Aizu in 1868. During this battle, Takeko led her fellow women warriors in a charge against the advancing Imperial Army .Her bravery became legendary, and she is remembered today as one of Japan's last female samurai.

The Joshitai's story is inspiring for its courage and commitment, showcasing the role of women in Japanese history during a period of immense change. Their stand was one of the last efforts to preserve the samurai way of life, which would soon fade with the modernization and unification of Japan under the Meiji government. Here are a few notable members of the women's army, especially those involved in the Aizu defense during the Boshin War:

Nakano Takeko – The most famous leader of the Joshitai, Takeko was a skilled martial artist and spear fighter. Takeko died in battle, but she remains a symbol of courage and the fierce fighting spirit of the women of the Aizu clan.

Tomioka Kōrin – Another notable woman who fought during the Boshin War, although much less is known about her life compared to Nakano Takeko. She was part of the Joshitai and participated in the defense of Aizu.

Yamada Hikaru – A member of the Joshitai who fought alongside Nakano Takeko. Hikaru was one of the many women who stepped up to defend Aizu during its final moments of resistance.

While there were several women who participated in the defense of Aizu, the majority of the Joshitai consisted of women from samurai families, many of whom were trained in various forms of combat, including archery, spear fighting, and swordsmanship.

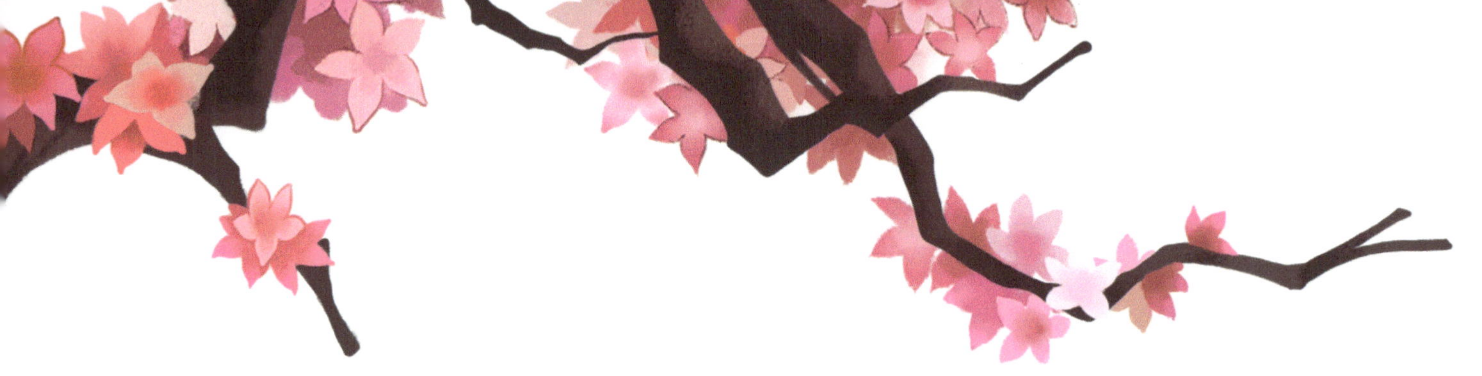

HER BRAVERY.

HER ULTIMATE SACRIFICE.

HER PASSION FOR HER PEOPLE.

Nakano Takeko was the leader of the Joshitai, a group of brave female warriors during Japan's Boshin War. To learn more about the Joshitai, please subscribe here:

https://aidazaciragic.com

SUPPORT HER LEGACY.
SUPPORT WOMEN EVERYDAY.

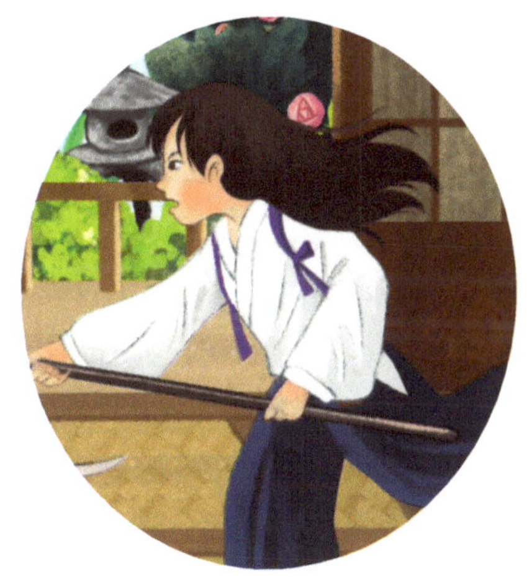

Help us spread the word of Takeko's incredible sacrifice and legacy.

Please consider leaving a review on any platform (Amazon, Goodreads, etc) to encourage others to read this book and support the mission. Scan the QR code below to visit my author hopmepage and discover more books about amazing women of the past.

About Aida

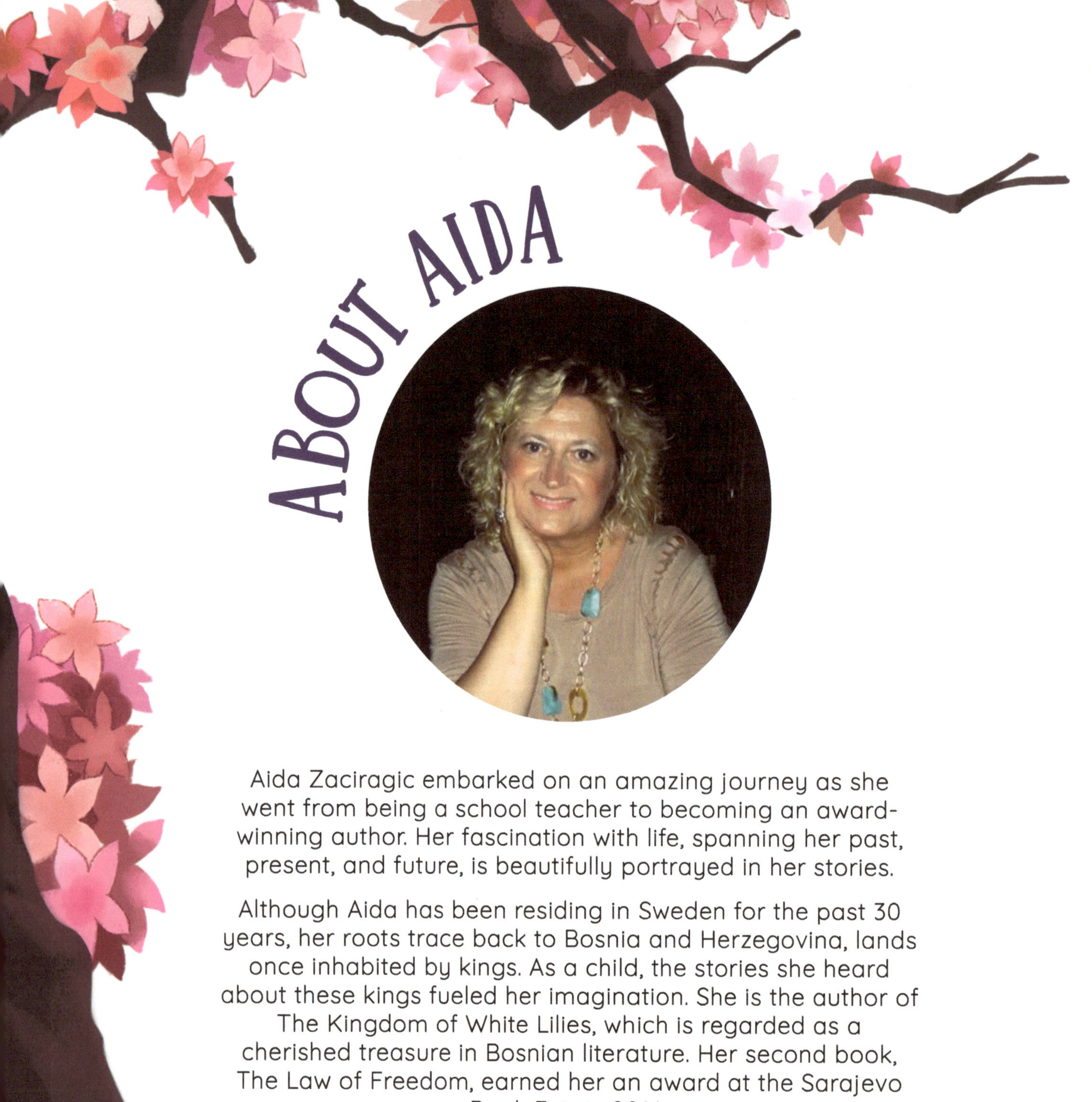

Aida Zaciragic embarked on an amazing journey as she went from being a school teacher to becoming an award-winning author. Her fascination with life, spanning her past, present, and future, is beautifully portrayed in her stories.

Although Aida has been residing in Sweden for the past 30 years, her roots trace back to Bosnia and Herzegovina, lands once inhabited by kings. As a child, the stories she heard about these kings fueled her imagination. She is the author of The Kingdom of White Lilies, which is regarded as a cherished treasure in Bosnian literature. Her second book, The Law of Freedom, earned her an award at the Sarajevo Book Fair in 2014.

Look for More Stories of Influential Women from the Author

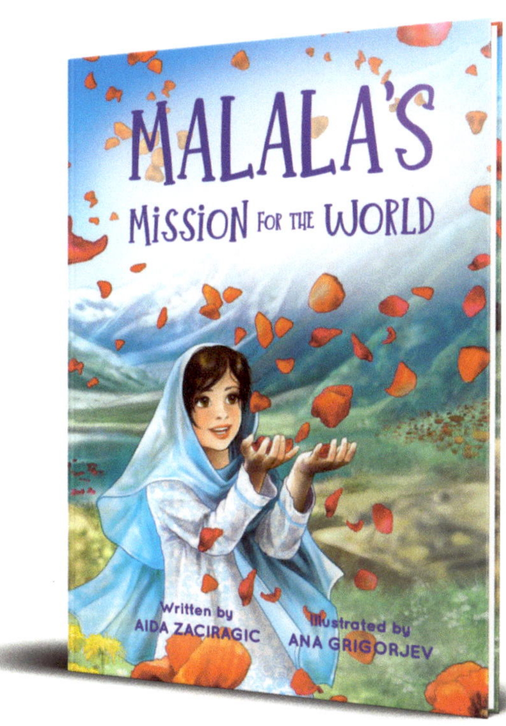